W9-DCR-632

Seeking Wisdom

THROUGH THE PROVERBS IN A YEAR

Copyright © 2017 by Stephanie Schwartz

All rights reserved. No part of this book may be used or reproduced in any manner whatsoever without written permission of the publisher, except for brief quotations in reviews or articles.

Scripture quotations are from The Holy Bible, English Standard Version® (ESV®), copyright © 2001 by Crossway, a publishing ministry of Good News Publishers. Used by permission.
All rights reserved.

ISBN 978-0-9986274-0-3

Compass Bible Church
150 Columbia
Aliso Viejo, CA 92656
949.540.0699
www.CompassChurch.org

Thank You

Thank you to Jennifer Morris for humbly editing these entries, Evie Mayer for being the best assistant, and Ruth Staggs for your faithful friendship.

Introduction:

We are faced with decisions every day. Some of them are small and won't make much of a difference even a day or two from now, while others are significant, and may alter the course of our lives or the lives of those we love. We all need wisdom to make good choices, sound judgments, and to select the best paths as we navigate the journeys of our lives. What better place to get wisdom than the ancient and inspired book of Proverbs!

My prayer is that as we carefully read and re-read this book, thinking about what the text of Scripture meant to the original audience, and applying its truths to our lives, we will become women who draw closer to the ultimate author of the Proverbs, the Lord and God of the Universe. As we seek God's wisdom through the book of Proverbs, may we travel through this life with minimal regrets and maximum success.

-Stephanie Schwartz
Director of Women's Ministry
Compass Bible Church

The proverbs of Solomon,
son of David, king of Israel:
To know wisdom and instruction,
to understand words of insight,

Proverbs 1:1-2 ESV

The book of Proverbs begins with its title: the proverbs of Solomon. He was the last king to reign over all of Israel, and took the seat of his father David. Unlike other texts found in the ancient Near East, this book begins with no specific addressee and is directed toward Israel as a whole. The first declared goal of Proverbs is to know wisdom and instruction. The Hebrew word for "to know" means "to become aware of," which can't be achieved without putting wisdom into practice. Instruction involves correction. If we really want to become wise, we have to be teachable. We must be willing to submit ourselves to an authority or source higher than ourselves and make changes when we are wrong. We either respond to wisdom or we don't, and if we don't, we have no one to blame but ourselves. Will you be more teachable this year than you were last year?

to receive instruction in wise dealing in righteousness, justice, and equity; to give prudence to the simple, knowledge and discretion to the youth—

Proverbs 1:3-4 ESV

The student must accept instruction, which gives way to the goal of the proverbs: wise behavior. The community as a whole benefits when its members learn to act rightly, justly, and fairly. Often, when we engage in thoughtful conversation, taking the time to learn what others are struggling with and listening to their outlook on things, we become more likely to empathize with them, even extending them proper respect, although we may disagree. The wise teacher is called to help the simple or gullible become shrewd. The naïve need life experience to gain wisdom. In what area do you struggle with good decision-making? Do you tend to believe accounts that most others would easily recognize as untrue? Let your knowledge of Scripture and life experience help you become more cautious before buying into the next error that seeks to mislead you. Stop, think, pray, and ask questions before you jump to conclusions today.

Let the wise hear and increase in learning, and the one who understands obtain guidance, to understand a proverb and a saying, the words of the wise and their riddles. The fear of the Lord is the beginning of knowledge; fools despise wisdom and instruction.

Proverbs 1:5-7 ESV

"Understanding" is repeated twice as a reminder that hard work and study are essential to wisdom. A proverb is like a parable, and the words of the wise and their riddles impart proven statements that require careful thought and consideration. Verse 7 is the foundation of the entire book. Practically, this is where the foolish and the wise are separated. The fool wants to live according to her own desires and pleasures. The one who is wise, on the other hand, lives with a continual awareness of the existence of God and his right to oversee and manage all of creation. The wise one trusts that God's choices are better than her own choices, and will align herself with his will. Do you ever feel like obedience to God is going to leave you wanting or cheated? It's not. In fact, the opposite is true. God knows what's best for us. We need to listen to and apply what he says.

Hear, my son, your father's instruction, and forsake not your mother's teaching, for they are a graceful garland for your head and pendants for your neck.

Proverbs 1:8-9 ESV

Solomon addressed the hearer as his son, but since no specific name was given, his wisdom was to be passed from Israel's parents to her children, and ultimately from God to his followers. The son is charged with holding on to his parents' teaching. Why? The instruction and teaching of his parents are like a garland or victor's crown for his head and a pendant for his neck. In the ancient Near East, the garland was a symbol of high social status, and the pendant was worn as a sign of protection. Though we may not wear garlands and pendants, if we apply the teaching of the Lord to our lives, we will appear different from those around us. When we make decisions consistent with God's law and principles those choices display to the watching world that we belong to Jesus. How does the world view you? Are you seen as a set apart daughter of the King? If not, what change can you make today?

5

My son, if sinners entice you, do not consent. If they say, "Come with us, let us lie in wait for blood; let us ambush the innocent without reason; like Sheol let us swallow them alive, and whole, like those who go down to the pit;

Proverbs 1:10-12 ESV

The son is advised to reject the way of those who violate God's standard for human behavior. Even in the ancient days of Solomon, sinners sought to persuade others to follow along with them as they preyed upon the innocent. They would wait for an unsuspecting victim and kill him to amuse themselves. They were motivated by hell and in league with death itself. So why do "sinners love company"? Why did these men want others to join them in the darkness? When those who live in disobedience recruit others to do the same, they feel less responsible for their transgression, and can say, "Everyone is doing it. It's not just me." Though we may not be included in the group of "cool" people, let's listen to wisdom's warning and say "no" to those who pressure us to compromise what we know is right. What can you do to become better at letting others know you are more concerned with God's opinion than man's?

we shall find all precious goods,
we shall fill our houses with plunder;
throw in your lot among us; we will all
have one purse"—

Proverbs 1:13-14 ESV

The sinners enticed others to join them by making promises of financial gain. In joining the "gang," all sorts of precious things would belong to the members. What temptation for the one who struggled to earn a day's living! If he turned to the dark side, he could be financially set. In fact, with a community purse, none would go without. There was surely more to be gained by exploiting others with the group. Though we may not murder one another to get each other's stuff, many still use relationships for personal benefit. Those who live for themselves see other people as commodities to be exploited. They look at others and think, "What can I get from this relationship? How will this 'friendship' benefit me?" Do you use people to serve your own agenda? Or do you share what God has graced you with and invest into others? Make sure you are willing to give in proportion to what you have received.

my son, do not walk in the way with them; hold back your foot from their paths, for their feet run to evil, and they make haste to shed blood.

Proverbs 1:15-16 ESV

Solomon warned his son not to walk in the way of those who do evil. The Hebrew word for "way," *derek*, includes both a lifestyle and the consequences of living that lifestyle. Then the father told his son to hold back his foot, or restrain himself, from the temptation to even experiment with sinful practices. Rebellion is addicting, and those who taste it often end up enslaved by it. The feet of the wrongdoers run to evil because of their bondage to it, they simply can't resist its deceptive lure. The wicked are quick to shed blood, which includes the life of their victims and their own lives as well. Are you currently experimenting with any thoughts or behaviors that you know are displeasing to God? If so, do whatever it takes to put an end to them. It has rightly been said, "Sin leads you further than you ever thought you would stray. Sin keeps you longer than you ever thought you would stay. And sin costs you more than you ever thought you would pay."

For in vain is a net spread in the sight of any bird, but these men lie in wait for their own blood; they set an ambush for their own lives. Such are the ways of everyone who is greedy for unjust gain; it takes away the life of its possessors.

Proverbs 1:17-19 ESV

God has given the birds insight so that when they see a trapper's net, they avoid it. So the hunter must sneak up behind the birds and throw his net over their heads to capture them. But sinners aren't as smart as the birds. They can see the bondage of their habits and practices, yet they walk right into them! How foolish! Evildoers lose their own lives to the very behaviors they have chosen to participate in. Those who are greedy for unjust gain end up with nothing in the end. Sin is always followed by consequences, and the momentary pleasures of wickedness pale in comparison to the devastating effects of ungodly living. We are faced with choices every day. Will we walk into bad behavior, or will we fly from it like the birds? What self-indulgent desires must you run from to avoid sin's traps today?

Wisdom cries aloud in the street, in the markets she raises her voice; at the head of the noisy streets she cries out; at the entrance of the city gates she speaks:

Proverbs 1:20-21 ESV

Wisdom makes every effort to reach as many people as possible. She doesn't hide in a closet at home, but she cries aloud and raises her voice in public places. She is zealous about her message and longs for people to respond to her teaching. She even goes to the head of the streets and the entrance of the city gate to warn those who arrive in town about the plan of evildoers to entice and seduce the naïve into following after sinful ways. Clearly, wisdom is available for all who desire her. If we ignore wisdom, we can't say her advice wasn't available. When we don't want to be told what to do, we end up missing wisdom. Does it bother you when people are fervent about obedience to God? Do you wish they would just "mind their own business?" Wisdom often speaks through others. Ask the people around you what they think about your inner struggles. You may be pleasantly surprised by their input and advice.

"How long, O simple ones, will you love being simple? How long will scoffers delight in their scoffing and fools hate knowledge? If you turn at my reproof, behold, I will pour out my spirit to you; I will make my words known to you.

Proverbs 1:22-23 ESV

In an almost exhausted fashion, wisdom again cries out, "How long?!" How much longer until the simple are done being naïve? Living without wisdom is acceptable for the very young, but not for those who have passed out of childhood. Yet many still love the fleeting pleasures of sin and refuse to repent from gross disobedience. So wisdom makes her appeal one more time, saying, "turn at my reproof." If one repents, then wisdom will respond. But remember, the opportunity will not always be available. When those who scoff at knowledge continue to spurn her plea, they will eventually be given over to their hard hearts. Sadly, in our culture, parents want to be like their kids, rather than the other way around. In what area are you living immaturely, like a child, whose primary concern is the gratification of selfish desires? Put an end to this silly thinking today! Those who *are* women should *behave* like women. Embrace discipline, grow up, and be someone others will look up to rather than down at.

Because I have called and you refused to listen, have stretched out my hand and no one has heeded, because you have ignored all my counsel and would have none of my reproof, I also will laugh at your calamity; I will mock when terror strikes you,

Proverbs 1:24-26 ESV

Though wisdom passionately desires a genuine listening audience, she is ignored. And consequences result. Her words of advice are disregarded by the naïve. She attemps to reason with the foolish and gullible, but they make no effort to even save their own lives. Because of this, she will laugh when what she warned about comes to pass. She will see and say to herself, "I told you, but you did not listen." The calamity and terror will come suddenly and unexpected, though the fool should know better. The Bible clearly instructs us in how to live wisely. If we ignore Scripture's warning by mistreating our physical bodies, abusing our finances, neglecting relationships, tolerating greed and selfishness, or even spurning opportunities to know and serve the Lord, we will experience regrets. If you died right now, what would you wish you had done differently? Why not make the change today?

when terror strikes you like a storm and
your calamity comes like a whirlwind,
when distress and anguish come upon you.
Then they will call upon me, but I will
not answer; they will seek me diligently
but will not find me.

Proverbs 1:27-28 ESV

Wisdom again declares what will occur if she continues to be rejected. She doesn't reveal exactly what the source of the terror, calamity, distress, and anguish will be, but the guarantees that the deeds of those who refuse her will catch up with them. In fact, the Day is coming when all that is wrong will be made right and those who defy God will be overturned, exposed, and humiliated. In the end, just as wisdom called to her audience and was ignored, she will be called upon, but she will be the one who ignores. Although many tend to forget, the opportunity for repentance will one day pass. So wisdom does whatever she can to shake up the naïve. Let's not miss the compassion wisdom extends to the simple. She begs for a listening ear. In what area are you resisting her promptings? Be wise and give in today! Wisdom wants nothing but the best for you.

Because they hated knowledge and did not choose the fear of the Lord, would have none of my counsel and despised all my reproof, therefore they shall eat the fruit of their way, and have their fill of their own devices.

Proverbs 1:29-31 ESV

Wisdom stresses the reason that judgment comes. The fools did not fear the Lord. By rejecting wisdom, they rejected God as well. "Hating," "choosing," and "despising" imply something willfully done. Wisdom reminds her audience that there is nothing unfair about judgment. The fools received exactly what they wanted. They longed to live according to their own desires: without wisdom and without God. In the end, they will get what they yearned for: eternity without wisdom and shut out from the presence of the Lord. Those who push God out of their lives choose to do so. Many will irrationally try to live without wisdom in just some areas of life. But God desires to rule over our whole person and not just part. Are there any aspects of your life that you don't want God "messing with"? If so, repent and allow him to be the Lord over all that you think and do.

> *For the simple are killed by their turning away, and the complacency of fools destroys them; but whoever listens to me will dwell secure and will be at ease, without dread of disaster."*

Proverbs 1:32-33 ESV

Those who are simple and foolish are doomed. Lulled into complacency by a false sense of security, they suffer the consequences of their wrong beliefs. On the other hand, all who listen to wisdom will be eternally secure. The wise don't turn away from the voice of God, but instead turn to Scripture, hearing and applying its instruction. All those who put their trust in God will never be disappointed. The simple and the foolish put their hope in what can be taken away. Those who trust in riches, beauty, pleasure, or power will one day find themselves destitute when the things they depend upon no longer provide for them. If you have lived foolishly, humble your heart before God and ask him for his wisdom. Then ask for courage to do as you should. Today could be the beginning of a brand new life for you.

My son, if you receive my words and treasure up my commandments with you, making your ear attentive to wisdom and inclining your heart to understanding;

Proverbs 2:1-2 ESV

The father began another address to his son and instructed him to prize the commandments. Since all wisdom comes from God, the commands of wisdom are actually the commands of God. Solomon, the father, was given the honor of building God's temple. The Ten Commandments were stored in the Ark of the Covenant, housed deep within the temple in the Most Holy Place. So Solomon said his son should be like the temple and hide the commands of the Lord within his own heart. We all protect and safely keep the things we treasure most. The son was to keep the word of God safe within himself. Do you read through the Bible quickly, just to check the box and say, "It's done!" Or is the word of God literally hidden within your heart? Let's not only read, but let's memorize the Bible as well. What changes can you make to become more effective at treasuring up the Scripture?

yes, if you call out for insight and raise your voice for understanding, if you seek it like silver and search for it as for hidden treasures, then you will understand the fear of the Lord and find the knowledge of God.

Proverbs 2:3-5 ESV

The exhortation moves from the passive, or what the son should hear, to the active, or what the son should pursue. The learner must call out and raise his voice for wisdom. And if he does, seeking wisdom like gold, or silver, or something worth a lot of money, he will be paid well. Those who ignore wisdom will face judgment, but those who seek wisdom will be blessed. The son will understand the fear of the Lord. The Scriptures teach that those who lack wisdom should ask for it from God. He promises to enlighten all who cry out for wisdom in faith. How intensely do you beg the Lord for insight? Do you seek good advice as intently as you would a lost cell phone or a lost wedding ring? God promises that those who turn to him, longing for and looking for wisdom, will be rewarded.

January

For the Lord gives wisdom; from his mouth come knowledge and understanding; he stores up sound wisdom for the upright; he is a shield to those who walk in integrity, guarding the paths of justice and watching over the way of his saints.

Proverbs 2:6-8 ESV

God spoke through Solomon to his son and to all of Israel. Because the student pursued wisdom, the Lord gave it to him. Listening to and applying wisdom protects the one who obeys like a shield protects a warrior. When God's instructions are put into practice, his children are kept safe from destruction. In fact, the Lord himself is a shield for his saints. He watches over their ways, preserving them in the midst of a crooked and dark world. "To watch over" includes guarding and nurturing. God ensures the spiritual safety of those who belong to him. How amazing to think that God is intimately involved with every detail in the lives of his people. Nothing catches him by surprise. Are you feeling troubled or insecure today? If you know the Lord, you have no need to fear. You are in the safest place in the universe.

Then you will understand righteousness and justice and equity, every good path; for wisdom will come into your heart, and knowledge will be pleasant to your soul; discretion will watch over you, understanding will guard you,

---

Proverbs 2:9-11 ESV

Because God gave the son wisdom, he could now discern between good and evil. The Hebrew word translated "path" describes the tracks left when wagon wheels moved through the mud. When those wet ruts dried out and hardened, a path remained. Wisdom leads the hearer down the right track. When a soul surrenders to God, the Lord graces her with a new heart. She is changed from the inside out and longs for the good way. As her new character matures, she makes better decisions with the choices she is presented with. Once on a path, it can be extremely difficult to get out of the rut. Bad habits are tough to break, but when we call out to God, he can lift us up, reposition us, and give us a new start. Why not get on a new and good track in one area of your life today? May your first steps lead to a lasting pattern of right behavior.

delivering you from the way of evil, from men of perverted speech, who forsake the paths of uprightness to walk in the ways of darkness, who rejoice in doing evil and delight in the perverseness of evil,

---

Proverbs 2:12-14 ESV

The son's maturity and knowledge will liberate him from the corruption of the world and from the manipulative, persuasive speech of those who turn wrong into right and right into wrong. The son will encounter people who attempt to lure him over to a life of darkness by persuading him that there's nothing sinful in what they are doing. They insist the way of the wicked is far more pleasurable than living uprightly. As you seek a God honoring life of wisdom, you too will encounter people who passionately insist that the things you know to be wicked are just fine. They will say, "Times have changed! God doesn't care about the things you're concerned about anymore. Everyone is doing it. Relax. It's really no big deal." But they are wrong. God does care. Speak the truth in love, and resist the world's plea to join with it today.

men whose paths are crooked, and who are devious in their ways. So you will be delivered from the forbidden woman, from the adulteress with her smooth words,

---

Proverbs 2:15-16 ESV

Men who seek to persuade the son away from wisdom are on crooked paths. Their practices deviate from the ways of the righteous, and self is the driving force behind all they do. The father alerts his son regarding the forbidden woman. Her flattering words long to deceive him, but wisdom will keep him from her trap. Her words are smooth. They promise pleasure and satisfaction, but their end is destruction. Our culture applauds sex outside of marriage and even pities those who submit their desires to God's law, but the Lord's standards provide us with protection. God authored sex, and he knows how to control its beautiful power in a way that honors him and the participants. Physical intimacy belongs to those who have entered into the covenant of marriage. If your guy isn't ready to be your husband, he's not ready to have your body. God is concerned with who you are and what you do.

*who forsakes the companion of her
youth and forgets the covenant of her
God; for her house sinks down to death,
and her paths to the departed; none
who go to her come back, nor do they
regain the paths of life.*

Proverbs 2:17-19 ESV

Although the forbidden woman has a husband, maybe even a godly man, she has no regard for her commitment to him. Though God witnessed their marriage vows, she doesn't care. She thinks God is withholding pleasure from her and pursues sex outside of her marriage. But her ways lead to death, and she drags those who are lured into her trap along with her. Sexual sin has devastating consequences, and those who enter into it will never be the same. It affects the entire person: physically, emotionally, and spiritually. If you have participated in extra-marital sex, see the seriousness of going outside of God's design. And yet, for all wrongdoers, there is hope in Christ. Jesus is willing to pay the penalty for your wrongdoing and wash away your stain, making you brand new if you confess your sin, trusting in him. Remember, what you do with your body matters to God.

So you will walk in the way of the good and keep to the paths of the righteous. For the upright will inhabit the land, and those with integrity will remain in it, but the wicked will be cut off from the land, and the treacherous will be rooted out of it.

Proverbs 2:20-22 ESV

In contrast to sinful ways that lead to death, the one who puts wisdom into practice will walk along the good paths that God designed for the righteous. Those who live in darkness will be removed from the goodness of the land, and only those who are upright will be allowed to remain. The Lord himself will cut off the ungodly, and he will ultimately restore all things to the way they are supposed to be. God has allowed men and women to dwell on earth and enjoy its blessings, but most have existed selfishly and rejected the authority of God over their lives. Though it may seem like they are prospering without the Lord, there will come a day when God makes all things right. Until then, don't grow weary in doing what you know the Lord has called you to do. God's timing is perfect, and he will straighten everything out soon.

My son, do not forget my teaching, but let your heart keep my commandments, for length of days and years of life and peace they will add to you.

Proverbs 3:1-2 ESV

The father encourages his son not to forget the teaching he has provided him with through the collection of proverbs. Although we learn something, we can "forget" what we know when we choose to live contrary to the teaching we received. If the son holds fast to the words he has memorized and meditated on, his life will be characterized by peace. The life he lives will be honest as he walks in fellowship with the Lord. To live a long life without God can be dark and depressing, but knowing God and communing with him brings peace that surpasses all circumstances. May we never forget that God's commandments are not burdensome. He doesn't call us to live in obedience to him to earn our salvation. An obedient life is a gift from God. It is an honor and a privilege to have his commands and to keep them.

Let not steadfast love and faithfulness forsake you; bind them around your neck; write them on the tablet of your heart. So you will find favor and good success in the sight of God and man.

Proverbs 3:3-4 ESV

The father associates his commandments with steadfast love and faithfulness. What a contrast between the way of wisdom and the way of the wicked, characterized by evil and selfishness! The son is not to forget the laws of God. He is to wear the truths he has learned and memorized like a protective necklace, which when put into practice, ward off unrighteousness. He will receive grace in this life and the life to come and be recognized by the community as one with a good reputation. Though we don't live for the approval of man, it is important that if we are rejected, our rejection not stem from our indulgence in sinful practices. The wise are people of whom others think highly of because of their commitment to virtuous behavior. How would those closest to you describe your character? Why not ask? If there are areas you need to change, then do so today.

Trust in the Lord with all your heart, and do not lean on your own understanding. In all your ways acknowledge him, and he will make straight your paths.

Proverbs 3:5-6 ESV

The son must place his confidence in the God who rules over all of creation, orchestrates every molecule in alignment with his good and sovereign plan, and is faithful to his promises. He must learn to depend on the Lord even more than he depends upon himself, including his own skills, talents, or abilities. The wise woman is called to acknowledge God's ultimate authority to reign and rule over every aspect of her life, as nothing escapes the notice of the Lord. As we yield to the laws and principles of the Scripture, our journey becomes straighter, smoother, and more consistent with God's intent for human life. A straight path isn't necessarily one without bumps along the way, but a course that ends in righteousness and blessing. One is a fool to believe her cleverness surpasses the intellect of the Lord. Be wise: abandon your fears, doubts, and insecurities by fully trusting in his word today.

Be not wise in your own eyes; fear the Lord, and turn away from evil. It will be healing to your flesh and refreshment to your bones. Honor the Lord with your wealth and with the firstfruits of all your produce; then your barns will be filled with plenty, and your vats will be bursting with wine.

Proverbs 3:7-10 ESV

God calls us to trust in his word rather than our own wisdom or cleverness. A healthy respect for the Lord causes us to steer clear of evil. We can forget that sin affects both our souls and our bodies. Spiritual and physical refreshment are the fruits of godly living, and those who are right with the Lord are emotionally healthy. Out of devotion to God, those who love him will offer to him their best. They give liberally from their finances, their time and their affections. God always outdoes those who are generous with him and causes them to prosper by providing all that is necessary and more. Do you give to God from your best? Do you long for daily time with him and anticipate opportunities to honor him and serve him by investing in your church? If not, ask the Lord to grace you with passion for him and for the people he loves.

My son, do not despise the Lord's discipline or be weary of his reproof, for the Lord reproves him whom he loves, as a father the son in whom he delights.

Proverbs 3:11-12 ESV

God uses discipline to correct his people. The point of the discipline is to deliver from foolishness, so correction should be embraced and not rejected. In fact, discipline is actually a sign of God's love and mercy. Just like a parent disciplines her children, the Lord disciplines those who belong to him. In fact, it's been said that to reject the discipline of the Lord is to reject his love. The caring father desires that his son experience the benefits of living according to wisdom, and he will do what he can to help his son get on and stay on the right path. Are you experiencing the discipline of the Lord? If so, change your attitude and actions and resolve to do things his way. Not all pain is the result of discipline, but when it is, the quicker we respond to the correction of the Lord, the quicker the "spanking" stops.

Blessed is the one who finds wisdom, and the one who gets understanding, for the gain from her is better than gain from silver and her profit better than gold.

Proverbs 3:13-14 ESV

The Hebrew word used for "blessed" here describes an experience of life to the fullest. God prospers those who are blessed by gracing them with well-being. The one who searches for wisdom and finds her, or the one who listens to and accepts understanding, is the one whom the Lord deems as blessed. Wisdom acquired and lived out is superior to all the riches of the world. As the saying goes, "Money can't buy me love." The things the human soul really longs for, fellowship with God and trusting relationships with one another, are the byproducts of a wise life. What one thing do you truly desire from this life? Is it something that can be obtained by silver or gold? Probably not! Determine to find wisdom and get understanding by listening to and obeying the word of the Lord. Then you will have your heart's desires.

January

She is more precious than jewels, and nothing you desire can compare with her. Long life is in her right hand; in her left hand are riches and honor.

Proverbs 3:15-16 ESV

Wisdom is worth more than riches. Though money can buy "stuff," none can buy a relationship with God, good character, or the ability to live uprightly. The things most prized are priceless. "Precious" also implies that wisdom is rare. Many are foolish, but few know and follow after wisdom. The right hand of wisdom holds long life, and her left hand holds riches and honor. Life, on the right, is above wealth and dignity, yet they are the byproducts of a godly life. Even the scoffer will concede that those who live consistently with what they believe are worthy of respect. Whom do you consider wise? Do you desire to be numbered among the wise? Know that nothing in this life compares with wisdom, and be willing to forsake all to find her. You will not be disappointed.

Her ways are ways of pleasantness, and all her paths are peace. She is a tree of life to those who lay hold of her; those who hold her fast are called blessed.

Proverbs 3:17-18 ESV

Wisdom benefits the one who both listens to and puts her teachings into practice. As the student walks along the wise path, his soul is at peace. He is no longer at war with God. Ultimately, wisdom is life and healing to all who long for and cling to her. Because of their disobedience, Adam and Eve were excluded from the Garden of Eden and kept from the tree of life, but the one who confesses her sin and places her faith in Christ will have access to that tree again in the paradise of God. Even if you are struggling hard today, keep your thoughts on the things above. One day, those God has declared righteous will eat from the tree of life in heaven. The wonders that await the one who has abandoned herself to wisdom by following Jesus will surpass all that the mind can imagine.

The Lord by wisdom founded the earth; by understanding he established the heavens; by his knowledge the deeps broke open, and the clouds drop down the dew.

Proverbs 3:19-20 ESV

Through wisdom, God created the heavens and the earth. How magnificent to ponder the universe and then consider that God established it according to his wisdom. God has firmly fixed our planet in its place until he is ready to bring it to an end. In his wisdom, the Lord separated the moisture in the clouds from the seas and authored the life sustaining water cycle. But God didn't set things into motion and step back. Instead, he remains personally involved in all the details of his design. Because he is present in all places at all times, he upholds everything. God wants us to follow after his wisdom, which is the same wisdom that drove creation! One would have to be a fool to turn her back on God's offer to gain wisdom. Humble yourself before your creator today, ask for insight, and seek him in his word.

My son, do not lose sight of these — keep sound wisdom and discretion, and they will be life for your soul and adornment for your neck.

Proverbs 3:21-22 ESV

The father implores his son to take hold of his teachings. Though originally delivered in spoken form, we now have these teachings recorded for our understanding in the pages of Scripture. Not to lose sight requires that we continually give our attention to reading and meditating on God's words. The priority we give to the teaching of the Lord is worn like a jeweled necklace for all to see. It is an honor to have the instruction that comes directly from God. But the study of God's word is just the beginning. His teaching is only complete in us when we put it into practice. If we know and give sound advice, we need to follow it ourselves too. Is there any area in which you give great instruction to others, but fail to obey it in your own life? If so, determine to live consistently with what you know to be true.

Then you will walk on your way securely, and your foot will not stumble. If you lie down, you will not be afraid; when you lie down, your sleep will be sweet.

Proverbs 3:23-24 ESV

If the son follows the father's wise teaching, he will live in security. Whether he walks or lies down, he will be safe. At no time is he left unprotected. How can harm come to the one under the watchful eyes of the Lord? Those who live according to the Lord's commands will even sleep peacefully because they are sheltered by his great power and care. Does this mean nothing painful will ever come to the righteous? No. Those who love and obey God can and will suffer in this life, but nothing in all of creation is able to touch the soul of the woman who belongs to the Lord. And nothing takes God by surprise. Those who live wisely know that anything unpleasant that comes their way has been filtered through the loving hand of an all-powerful God.

Do not be afraid of sudden terror or of the ruin of the wicked, when it comes, for the Lord will be your confidence and will keep your foot from being caught.

Proverbs 3:25-26 ESV

The one who searches for, finds, and applies God's wisdom has no need to fear the impending and sudden disaster that will come upon the wicked, because the Lord will keep her safe. Even in the midst of judgment, God will shield those who are his from any and all spiritual harm. Think about Rahab, the prostitute or innkeeper of Jericho who put her trust in the God of Israel. Her home was actually built right into the wall that protected the city of Jericho. When God judged that ancient city, the most dangerous place in the world was where she lived, in the community's wall. And yet, although the wall collapsed, somehow the Lord kept Rahab and her family safe. Choose to embrace whatever God's wisdom is asking of you today. Even in the dark, God is with those who are his, every step of the way.

Do not withhold good from those to whom it is due, when it is in your power to do it. Do not say to your neighbor, "Go, and come again, tomorrow I will give it"— when you have it with you. Do not plan evil against your neighbor, who dwells trustingly beside you.

Proverbs 3:27-29 ESV

The wise are kind to others. When a woman living according to God's design has the ability to help, she does what she can. And she doesn't delay in offering aid. She will not make excuses, but instead gets involved immediately. She is never to take advantage of her trusting neighbor by scheming against him or devising ways to exploit him. The neighbor of the godly woman should feel secure living beside her. Wise people are not self-consumed but honestly look out for those around them. Both the friends and the neighbors of the wise woman know that when necessary, she will quickly come to their aid. What about you? Would others consider you a good neighbor? Do those around you sense you are watching out for them? If you are safe in the Lord, help others to feel secure by caring for them today.

Do not contend with a man for no reason, when he has done you no harm. Do not envy a man of violence and do not choose any of his ways, for the devious person is an abomination to the Lord, but the upright are in his confidence.

Proverbs 3:30-32 ESV

The godly person will not fabricate a grievance with those around her for attention or personal gain. The wise should never long for what the wicked person has. Although the ungodly may experience temporary pleasure and ease, the righteous person is not to covet the life of the evil man. God hates the ways of the wicked. The Lord sees all and distinguishes between the good and the evil neighbors. The evil neighbor seeks to harm, while the good neighbor experiences God's wisdom and is always ready to do what is right in the eyes of the Lord. If you live around ungodly people, who may even seem to have all the perks in life, don't envy them. One day they will be shut out from the presence of God forever. If your heart is aching for what others have, take a mental step back and get your perspective right today.

The Lord's curse is on the house of the wicked, but he blesses the dwelling of the righteous. Toward the scorners he is scornful, but to the humble he gives favor. The wise will inherit honor, but fools get disgrace.

Proverbs 3:33-35 ESV

God blesses the one who is righteous, including all that he has. At the same time, God rejects the wicked along with all that is valuable to him. God will mock those who mock the righteous. The wicked will reap what he sows as everything takes place under the watchful eye of the Lord. God will right all wrongs. The righteous who were mocked by the wicked will be graced with God's favor. Those who are wise will be given much from God, but fools will be associated with failure, especially as they leave this earth empty handed. Jesus asked, "For what will it profit a man if he gains the whole world and forfeits his soul?" How would you respond to Jesus' question? What on earth is worth the price of your soul? If anything is keeping you from wisdom today, choose to let it go.

Hear, O sons, a father's instruction, and be attentive, that you may gain insight, for I give you good precepts; do not forsake my teaching.

Proverbs 4:1-2 ESV

The father addresses his sons. This wisdom was not just for his immediate son, but for his grandsons and great-grandsons and so on. The sons are called to pay attention to his instruction because the father's teaching provided insight, which enabled the sons to function well in the family, the community, and before the Lord. How are you at listening to the advice of your parents, grandparents, and even great-grandparents? God often uses those who have lived longer to impart sound and practical truths to their offspring. Remember to filter the advice you receive through the lens of Scripture, but don't disregard the wisdom of those who have gone before you. And be prepared to pass the wisdom of the Lord on to your children, grandchildren, nieces, nephews, and even the children of your church. Those who have learned to blend biblical truth with life experience should share that knowledge with others.

When I was a son with my father, tender, the only one in the sight of my mother, he taught me and said to me, "Let your heart hold fast my words; keep my commandments and live. Get wisdom; get insight; do not forget, and do not turn away from the words of my mouth.

Proverbs 4:3-5 ESV

Now the father teaches what his father, the son's grandfather, said. Like the son, the father also depended upon his parents and listened to the sound instruction of his father. The grandfather taught his son to take hold of and obey his teaching so that the son might experience a good and honorable life. The grandfather put a high price tag on wisdom. The word translated "get" in verse 5 means "to acquire, gain possession of or buy." The son must be willing to sacrifice to become wise. If wisdom is not prized and sought after, then she will have no effect on the hearer. The grandfather's advice was the same as the father's advice: do not steer away from wisdom's path. What circumstances or people cause you to veer off the path of the wise? Prayerfully identify what those things are and choose to reduce their influence on your heart and mind today.

Do not forsake her, and she will keep you; love her, and she will guard you. The beginning of wisdom is this: Get wisdom, and whatever you get, get insight. Prize her highly, and she will exalt you; she will honor you if you embrace her. She will place on your head a graceful garland; she will bestow on you a beautiful crown."

Proverbs 4:6-9 ESV

The son is called to be faithful to and love wisdom. He is to set his desire upon obeying the commands of God. If the son is committed to wisdom, she will protect and guard him. Becoming wise begins with the right response to this question: how much do you want wisdom? If you don't really care, then wisdom is not for you. If you will do whatever it takes to obtain her, then she will be yours. If one holds wisdom close, she will be successful. And if one embraces wisdom, wisdom will bring her honor. Wisdom will place a beautiful victor's crown upon the head of the one who is faithful. The one who follows wisdom will be adorned with a garland that the whole world will see. Those who live biblically are graced with a beauty that never fades away. There's nothing more attractive than a life that has been lived according to God's design.

Hear, my son, and accept my words,
that the years of your life may be many.
I have taught you the way of wisdom; I
have led you in the paths of uprightness.

Proverbs 4:10-11 ESV

We are reminded that listening isn't enough. Application of truth is necessary to honestly embrace wisdom. When one chooses to obey the commands of God, her life will be full. She may not have the longest life, but it will certainly be a great life. The Hebrew word *derek* translated "way" and used continually in Proverbs, points to a whole lifestyle. The paths of uprightness are ancient courses which the godly have journeyed on for centuries. Let's not neglect our need to apply wisdom for another moment. What have you been telling yourself that you are "going to do" for days, weeks, months, or even years? Why wait? It really won't be easier to be obedient tomorrow than it is today. Now is the time to live out what you know is right. Let everyone see you walking on the path of wisdom in all that you think and all that you do.

When you walk, your step will not be hampered, and if you run, you will not stumble. Keep hold of instruction; do not let go; guard her, for she is your life.

Proverbs 4:12-13 ESV

Whether the obedient son walks or runs along the course of wisdom, his journey will be safe. Sinful entrapments that lead to stumbling are removed from the way of the one who lives according to wisdom. The father charges the son to keep hold of his instruction and never let go. The pursuit of wisdom is a life-long discipline. The one who seeks to be wise must be shrewd about where she focuses her energy and efforts. She is certainly not accustomed to ease or laziness. Do you feel worn out or tired? Fix your eyes upon Jesus today. Remember, he is our wisdom, he is our rest, and he provides us with the strength we need to do everything he's called us to. Don't grow weary, and don't let go! Ask God to empower you with all that you need to finish your course and finish it well.

Do not enter the path of the wicked, and do not walk in the way of the evil. Avoid it; do not go on it; turn away from it and pass on. For they cannot sleep unless they have done wrong; they are robbed of sleep unless they have made someone stumble.

Proverbs 4:14-16 ESV

The father implores the son to do whatever it takes to stay away from those who do evil. Six times in a row, he tells the son the same thing. Do not enter, do not walk in, avoid, do not go on, turn away, and pass on the path of the wicked. Clearly, those who are wise stay as far away from evil as possible. Only the fool thinks she can get close to darkness without being affected. The son is to pass on or keep walking without straying off the way of righteousness. Sin is so consuming that those who are entrapped by it can't even sleep until they have done wrong. The disobedient look forward to the darkness of night. As you journey along the course of righteousness, what tempts you to stop, look, and linger? Identify your weaknesses and determine to avoid anything that could lead you off track today.

For they eat the bread of wickedness and drink the wine of violence. But the path of the righteous is like the light of dawn, which shines brighter and brighter until full day. The way of the wicked is like deep darkness; they do not know over what they stumble.

Proverbs 4:17-19 ESV

Wickedness is normal for those who do evil. Violence results as evildoers seek to increase in pleasure and wealth. Their gain comes at the expense of others. Their hearts are hardened by sin. The wicked live in darkness and can't even find their way out. They fail to see the connection between their sin and its consequences in their lives. They don't believe their disobedience will result in eternal death. What a sad state for those who reject God's wisdom. But what hope for those who follow the Lord! While darkness reigns over evildoers, the light grows daily for those whose goal is Jesus. Soon we will be face to face with the one who loves us more than we could ever think or imagine. May our separation from darkness be more evident today than ever before. Let's determine to avoid sin at all costs, focusing our minds on that which is right and pure.

February
14

My son, be attentive to my words; incline your ear to my sayings. Let them not escape from your sight; keep them within your heart. For they are life to those who find them, and healing to all their flesh.

Proverbs 4:20-22 ESV

The father exhorts his son to pay attention to his teaching. The son must continually pursue the way of wisdom, reading over and obeying the commands of the Lord. This will require a lifetime of saying "no" to the desires of the sinful flesh and the pull of the world while actively walking along the path of the wise. But the reward will be great. We must all be healed from sin and its effects in our lives. It is through the supernatural work of the Lord that we are given new hearts and rewired to walk in his ways. Often the world around us tries to heal moral failure with medication or therapy, which may provide a temporary Band-Aid, but never really get to the cancer under the skin. Align your desires with the will of Jesus today. His Spirit will refresh your soul in a way no other person or thing can.

*Keep your heart with all vigilance,
for from it flow the springs of life.
Put away from you crooked speech,
and put devious talk far from you.*

Proverbs 4:23-24 ESV

The heart must be carefully guarded. What we do is motivated by our desires, so if we keep our hearts in check, our behavior will also be right. In fact, the direction of our lives is determined by the condition of our hearts. Along with the heart, the mouth must be kept under guard. Our speech betrays the state of our inner person. If one seeks wisdom, she must do away with lying, deceptive, insensitive, and even harmful words. Jesus said, "What comes out of the mouth proceeds from the heart, and this defiles a person." What words have been coming out of your mouth lately? Are they honest, encouraging, and loving? Or have they been deceitful, critical, and mean? Determine to speak in a way consistent with wisdom. The woman who chooses to do this will end up refining not only her words, but her heart as well.

Let your eyes look directly forward, and your gaze be straight before you. Ponder the path of your feet; then all your ways will be sure. Do not swerve to the right or to the left; turn your foot away from evil.

Proverbs 4:25-27 ESV

The one who desires wisdom must be careful about what she looks at. She should fix her eyes upon Jesus and what is consistent with his character without looking to the right or the left, including what the world has to "offer." To keep her feet walking on the right path, her eyes must continually watch for where to take the next step. Veering just a short distance off course can result in danger or disaster. The path of the righteous is decidedly different from the path of the wicked. We can't have one foot on each route. The wise woman continually looks ahead, keeping her mind on the things above. We are bombarded with distractions that attempt to keep us from our mission and goal in life. Let's put away anything that hinders us from being as spiritually productive as possible during our brief stay on earth.

*My son, be attentive to my wisdom;
incline your ear to my understanding,
that you may keep discretion, and
your lips may guard knowledge.*

Proverbs 5:1-2 ESV

The father exhorts the son to pay attention to his wisdom and his life experience. The goal of this charge concerns the son's speech. The son must be careful with respect to what he says. The wise are cautious with their words. They don't speak impulsively, driven by emotional reactions to circumstances, but instead they thoughtfully process the attitudes of their hearts through the Scripture and line up their speech in accordance with God's wisdom. So much damage can be done by careless words. And once the words are out there, they cannot be taken back. We can repent and seek forgiveness when we have spoken wrongly, but often the consequences of our careless speech lingers for months and even years. May we improve at quieting our hearts when our emotions run high. Let's ask God to help us think and think again before we speak today.

For the lips of a forbidden woman drip honey, and her speech is smoother than oil, but in the end she is bitter as wormwood, sharp as a two-edged sword.

Proverbs 5:3-4 ESV

The father strongly warns his son against the inevitability of crossing paths with women who want to lure him into sexual sin. Sex begins with speech, and the forbidden woman knows exactly what she's doing as she seeks to wear down her victim with continual flattery and charm. Although she promises great pleasure and may seem captivating for the moment, her end is death and destruction. The consequences of sexual sin are huge, and many foolish victims have paid for their actions for years and even decades. We must keep ourselves from the messages that would lead to sexual sin, even if it's only in our minds. If any books, TV shows, movies, magazines or Internet sites are enticing you to participate in sexual deviance, determine to put a stop to them today. God will judge those who don't play by his rules when it comes to sexual behavior.

Her feet go down to death; her steps follow the path to Sheol; she does not ponder the path of life; her ways wander, and she does not know it.

Proverbs 5:5-6 ESV

The father continues to warn his son about the consequences of going after the woman who attempts to lure him into sexual sin. If he follows after her, he follows her to death. She has left her husband to pursue sexual pleasure outside of her marriage. She lives in a state of moral darkness and in time loses her ability to distinguish between right and wrong. These ancient truths are hotly contested in our current culture. Many will insist that no one has the right to dictate what happens in our bedrooms. But the Scripture teaches that God is concerned about what we do behind closed doors. He cares very much about what goes on in our bedrooms. Though we may be frowned upon or even mocked for holding onto principles of biblical sexuality, let's stick with God's design and say "no" to those who would try to persuade us otherwise.

And now, O sons, listen to me, and do not depart from the words of my mouth. Keep your way far from her, and do not go near the door of her house, lest you give your honor to others and your years to the merciless.

Proverbs 5:7-9 ESV

The father addresses his son, his grandsons, his great-grandsons, and so on, warning them about the destruction that sexual sin generates. Sex itself is not a sin. God is the one who created it and designed it to produce great pleasure. But like a fire, sex can devour when it blazes outside of the fireplace. When sex is practiced within God's parameters, it is not only beautiful, but it can bring glory to him. So we must continue to resist and stand far away from the things that tempt us to sin in this area. In particular, for those who are married, the price tag associated with adultery can be unbearable. Many young and healthy marriages are marred for years and years by marital unfaithfulness. If you are currently drawn to any form of sexual deviance, do whatever you can to overcome this temptation, even if it means confessing it to the whole church and asking for help.

lest strangers take their fill of your strength, and your labors go to the house of a foreigner, and at the end of your life you groan, when your flesh and body are consumed, and you say, "How I hated discipline, and my heart despised reproof!

Proverbs 5:10-12 ESV

If the son does not listen to the father's wisdom, he will suffer consequences. Earlier, the father warned about evildoers who sought to take whatever they could from their victims. But in the case of sex outside of God's design, if the son rejects the father's counsel, he will be a victim, but a victim of his own sinful choices. Jealousy, bitterness, anger, loneliness, depression, loss of reputation, disease, and financial burdens are some of the price tags that accompany sexual sin. The son is responsible to turn from temptation, and in the end, if he succumbs, it is because of his own lusts. He cannot blame it on anyone other than himself. Although the temptress, or the one who lures another into sexual sin, will give an account for her evil actions, the person who yields to her will not be able to shift blame when standing before the throne of God.

> *I did not listen to the voice of my teachers or incline my ear to my instructors. I am at the brink of utter ruin in the assembled congregation."*

Proverbs 5:13-14 ESV

The multiple voices of wisdom that warned against the severe consequences of turning to the forbidden woman were rejected. The sinner confessed his wrongdoing and lamented all that he lost as a result. Now his shame had reached the public arena. The facts were out in the open, exposed in the light, and there was no way to retract what had so foolishly been done in darkness. May we remember that even with two "consenting" adults, sexual sin affects more than just the pair. Spouses, children, parents, siblings, neighbors, and even co-workers are often crushed to learn of a friend or family member's unfaithfulness. Currently, pornography is at an all-time high. The Internet has opened doors to all sorts of darkness, and it's only a couple clicks away from anyone with a phone or computer. If you are viewing pornography, get help today. Call a godly friend and ask for immediate accountability.

Drink water from your own cistern, flowing water from your own well. Should your springs be scattered abroad, streams of water in the streets? Let them be for yourself alone, and not for strangers with you.

Proverbs 5:15-17 ESV

Instead of going to the forbidden woman, the father exhorts his son to satisfy his sexual thirst by drinking water from his own cistern, or going to his own wife for pleasure. A cistern, or a well for storing rainwater, was a prized and privately owned possession. The son should view his wife with high regard and turn to her alone for sexual gratification. This one flesh relationship was to occur solely between the husband and his wife. Are you single today? If so, wait until you are married to become sexually active. Are you married today? If so, no matter how tired, bored, or even disappointed you are with your spouse, keep your sexual relationship alive. Those who are married should do whatever they can to be sexually active. Plan time for sex with your spouse, think about sex with your spouse, and thoroughly enjoy the sexual aspect of your relationship with your spouse.

Let your fountain be blessed, and rejoice in the wife of your youth, a lovely deer, a graceful doe. Let her breasts fill you at all times with delight; be intoxicated always in her love. Why should you be intoxicated, my son, with a forbidden woman and embrace the bosom of an adulteress?

Proverbs 5:18-20 ESV

The father prays that his son's wife would satisfy his son's sexual thirst. The father's advice even points to the wisdom of marrying young, as he refers to the wife of his son's youth. The father encourages his son to fully enjoy sex with his wife. The pair should be free from insecurities and embarrassment as they participate together in the physical relationship God has called them to. In comparison to what God provides between the son and his wife, any so called pleasure he might get from a forbidden woman is not only foolish, but also evil and destructive. Can you imagine your father-in-law praying to God that you would be an abundant source of sexual satisfaction to your spouse? How are you doing in this area? Would the angels say you are the answer to his prayer? Or have you been withholding sex from your spouse? Maybe it's time to make some changes tonight.

For a man's ways are before the eyes of the Lord, and he ponders all his paths. The iniquities of the wicked ensnare him, and he is held fast in the cords of his sin. He dies for lack of discipline, and because of his great folly he is led astray.

Proverbs 5:21-23 ESV

Not only the one who practices sex outside of God's design, but all those disobedient to God's plan for humanity are under the watchful eye of the Lord. God sees in the light and in the dark. Like an animal caught in a hunter's trap is the woman who lives in darkness, enslaved by her sin. Having rejected wisdom, she walks toward her own death. God is aware of everything that occurs in the universe. He knows all there is to know, not only including what actually happens but what might happen as well. For those who reject the Lord, the omniscience of God should be a cause of great terror. But for those who have made peace with God through repentance and faith in his Son, his omniscience provides a source of extreme comfort. He alone knows the good that can and will come from even the most challenging circumstances.

My son, if you have put up security for your neighbor, have given your pledge for a stranger, if you are snared in the words of your mouth, caught in the words of your mouth, then do this, my son, and save yourself, for you have come into the hand of your neighbor: go, hasten, and plead urgently with your neighbor.

Proverbs 6:1-3 ESV

The father instructs his son about money and finances. The son is not to promise to cover another's debts. If the other party doesn't follow through with his payments, the cosigner, or the one who put up security, is obligated to pay all of what's owed. By guaranteeing to cover another's debts, the pledge has made a trap for him. He needs to do whatever he can to get out of the situation. How can you guarantee the one you have promised for will follow through on her contract? Do whatever you can, even to the point of exhausting yourself, to get out of the pledge situation. Even if you seem annoying, free yourself from any unwise financial agreements. Maybe you haven't cosigned for another, but you might be snared by foolish debt. If so, make it your priority to stop any avoidable spending until you can get out of unnecessary financial obligations.

Give your eyes no sleep and your eyelids no slumber; save yourself like a gazelle from the hand of the hunter, like a bird from the hand of the fowler.

Proverbs 6:4-5 ESV

The father explains the passion the son must exert to free himself from any foolish decision to put up a pledge for someone else's debts. The son should make this matter a top priority and not even sleep until he gets out of bad financial situations. Just as animals make every effort to escape the hunter's trap, so should the financial backer work to get out of the arrangement. Even if you are not a cosigner or a pledge for another's debts, any sizable financial decisions made without long and careful thought are to be avoided. If you have agreed to a financial contract and see the foolishness of your decision, get out of it immediately. And if you are obligated and can't be released, make it your priority to pay it off as quickly as possible. Think and think again before you sign on the next dotted line.

Go to the ant, O sluggard; consider her ways, and be wise. Without having any chief, officer, or ruler, she prepares her bread in summer and gathers her food in harvest.

Proverbs 6:6-8 ESV

Now the sluggard or the lazy person is addressed. He is to notice or pay attention to the ant. She labors to store her grain within her nest. Even though there is no leader over her to dictate deadlines and enforce a standard of excellence, she works diligently. Using her God given sense of wisdom, she prepares for the future. The ant realizes when it is harvest time, and she doesn't waste a moment. She does all she can to store up for the coming months so that she will not lack during the winter. Has God given you the ability to work or to serve him today? If so, don't waste your window of time. Like the ant, we are to make the most of every opportunity, because we don't know what tomorrow holds. Don't procrastinate, dragging today's duties to tomorrow's to-do list. Thank God for the gift of work, and get to it.

How long will you lie there, O sluggard? When will you arise from your sleep? A little sleep, a little slumber, a little folding of the hands to rest, and poverty will come upon you like a robber, and want like an armed man.

Proverbs 6:9-11 ESV

The sluggard must repent of his laziness before the harvest is gone and his opportunity to be productive has passed. He loves to rest, relax, and enjoy, so he fails to make the most of the time and season before him. But when will it be enough? Another day of sleeping in, another hour of useless activity, or another careless moment passes by and soon the sluggard has set the direction for the course of his life. He will experience the consequences of his behavior as poverty plunders his resources and takes from him whatever he may have. We should rest so that we can get back to work. Moses asked that God would teach us to number our days so that we may gain a heart of wisdom. Because our years on this planet are brief, the wise woman uses her time to advance the kingdom of God and invest in the life to come.

A worthless person, a wicked man, goes about with crooked speech, winks with his eyes, signals with his feet, points with his finger.

Proverbs 6:12-13 ESV

A troublemaker or a wicked person distorts the truth. Behind the back of the ones she seeks to ruin, her eyes let those around her know her evil intent. She shuffles her feet as another nonverbal sign, and even points out her victim to her associates. From her eyes all the way down to her feet, including her finger, the entire body of the unrighteous man or woman works to defame another. This troublemaker enjoys harming the reputation of the godly. She doesn't care about the ruin she may bring to another with her deceptive speech as long as she can be the center of attention. Stay away from those who seem to enjoy putting down others. In their desire to feel superior to those around them, they feel no shame as they cause others to look critically upon their victims. Never try to build yourself up by bringing others down.

with perverted heart devises evil,
continually sowing discord; therefore
calamity will come upon him suddenly; in a
moment he will be broken beyond healing.

Proverbs 6:14-15 ESV

The description of the wicked man continues. His evil behavior begins in his heart. He enjoys sabotaging the character of others and knows in advance how he plans to smear the reputation of his victims. He unleashes discord among communities of people, even the people of God. But God sees and will not allow this man to prosper in his disruptive ways. Instead, God will bring an abrupt end to his love of discord. This man will be laid low in this life and the life to come. Be forewarned: you will inevitably cross paths with this man. He badmouths those who are advancing the kingdom of God and manipulates others to make himself appear in the right. Stay away from the divisive man, lest you fall prey to his trap. Those that listen to him often don't see his selfish intentions until it is too late.

There are six things that the Lord hates, seven that are an abomination to him: haughty eyes, a lying tongue, and hands that shed innocent blood.

Proverbs 6:16-17 ESV

Because God is holy and will not tolerate unrighteous behavior, seven things are listed that he detests or separates himself from. The first are "haughty eyes." This phrase describes the one who arrogantly thinks she is superior to other humans and even above God. The prideful stand in opposition to the Lord. The second is a "lying tongue." God does not approve of those who use speech to communicate anything false. And the third are "hands that shed innocent blood." The wicked will do whatever it takes to get what they want. In which area do you struggle? Do you see yourself as superior to others? Do you deceive by including or omitting details, creating a picture that's not actually true? Or do you use people to get what you want? If you practice any of these things, repent and ask God to help you rid these traits from your life today.

a heart that devises wicked plans, feet that make haste to run to evil, a false witness who breathes out lies, and one who sows discord among brothers.

Proverbs 6:18-19 ESV

The final four of the seven things God hates are listed. The fourth is "a heart that devises wicked plans." This person thinks about and calculates how to effectively do wrong. "Feet that make haste to run to evil," the fifth in the list, describes this person's longing and hurriedness to follow through with her sinful plans. The sixth characteristic is a "false witness" who communicates things that simply are not true, and harms others as a result. And finally, in the seventh position, the climax of the list describes the person who disrupts family members, including those of a common community. All those who trust in the Lord rightly call God their Father, and God despises the actions of the one who creates friction between his people. When you run across this person, avoid her at all costs. Don't be foolishly allied with the woman who seeks to divide the children of God.

My son, keep your father's commandment, and forsake not your mother's teaching. Bind them on your heart always; tie them around your neck. When you walk, they will lead you; when you lie down, they will watch over you; and when you awake, they will talk with you.

Proverbs 6:20-22 ESV

The son is reminded to keep his parents' teaching, and ultimately, the command of the Lord. He is to memorize Scripture, doing whatever he can to keep the rule of the Lord in his heart and mind. Like a shepherd leads his sheep, the command of the Lord guides the way of the one obedient to his word. And as sheep need the shepherd's help to navigate through dangerous territories on their journey to pasture, so will the wise one need the wisdom of God's word to get through the troubles of this life. The wise son sleeps in safety and wakes up to eagerly learn and apply more from his teachers. Life in the ancient world was demanding, and life in the modern world has its share of difficulties too. But the word of the Lord remains throughout the ages. Determine to be directed by Scripture as you face life's challenges today.

For the commandment is a lamp and the teaching a light, and the reproofs of discipline are the way of life, to preserve you from the evil woman, from the smooth tongue of the adulteress.

Proverbs 6:23-24 ESV

The instructions of his parents provide the son with protection and guidance as he walks through life, keeping him from hidden dangers. Wisdom will shield the son from the adulteress, who has the potential to ruin life. Her speech is deceptive, and by her expert use of flattery, she successfully lures the naïve into her death trap. Families, careers, and reputations can be demolished as a result of giving in to her persuasive words. Maybe you feel impermeable to the lure of sexual sin. But adultery is crafty and can capture hearts and minds in a variety of ways. Is there someone down the street, at the gym, or at the office with whom you secretly entertain the thought of an affair? Do you escape from the mundane nature of your circumstances by fantasizing about someone new and different? If so, repent and fully embrace God's plan for your sexual behavior today.

Do not desire her beauty in your heart, and do not let her capture you with her eyelashes; for the price of a prostitute is only a loaf of bread, but a married woman hunts down a precious life. Can a man carry fire next to his chest and his clothes not be burned?

Proverbs 6:25-27 ESV

The admonition to keep the son from sexual sin continues. The adulteress uses her physical beauty to control her victims. She may be externally gorgeous, but God values inward beauty, and the son must resist the temptation to succumb to forbidden love because of outward appearance. Though a prostitute may only cost a few dollars, the price of violating the marriage oath carries a massive price tag. So is God validating the prostitute here? No! Instead, he is highlighting the exorbitant cost of adultery. The temporary pleasure is in no way worth what will be lost as a result. Many may feel their marriages have become stale and so may allow themselves to be attracted, even "just" emotionally, to someone other than their spouse. They believe that the "grass is greener" on the other side. This just isn't true. In fact, the grass is greener where it is watered the most. Invest in your own marriage today.

Or can one walk on hot coals and his feet not be scorched? So is he who goes in to his neighbor's wife; none who touches her will go unpunished.

Proverbs 6:28-29 ESV

The dangers associated with adultery continue. Just as charcoal, which melts metal and bakes food, would scorch a man's feet, so will he be burned by adultery. The effects of sexual sin are permanent, and God wants those who pursue wisdom to take sex outside of marriage extremely seriously. We must remember that God sees both our physical actions and our private thoughts. Because of our fallen nature, very few can say they've never sinned sexually, even within their minds. What's so amazing is that though sexual sin has consequences, Jesus died to pay the penalty for human sexual deviation before a holy and righteous God. If you agree that you don't have a spotless record when it comes to your sexuality, physically or mentally, then turn to Jesus. He is willing to take the punishment your transgressions have earned. Confess your sin, and ask God to make you as white as snow today.

People do not despise a thief if he steals to satisfy his appetite when he is hungry, but if he is caught, he will pay sevenfold; he will give all the goods of his house. He who commits adultery lacks sense; he who does it destroys himself.

Proverbs 6:30-32 ESV

People pity the thief who steals bread to satisfy physical hunger, but we should not feel sorry for the one who enters into forbidden sex to satisfy an appetite. The thief could repay the owner of the bread, making restitution for his wrong. But how does one repay for the crime of adultery? How is the violated spouse "bought off" when his wife has been taken by another? Adultery and sexual sin violate promises and boundaries, which just can't be undone or easily forgotten. If you are tempted to enter into sexual sin, call out to God for a way of escape. Contact a friend and get godly accountability. If your spouse has broken covenant with you, seek help. Pastors and leaders in your church want you to keep your marriage in tact. Don't sweep these things under the rug. Instead, be honest, and deal with sexual sin today.

He will get wounds and dishonor, and his disgrace will not be wiped away. For jealousy makes a man furious, and he will not spare when he takes revenge. He will accept no compensation; he will refuse though you multiply gifts.

Proverbs 6:33-35 ESV

The one who commits adultery will experience the disgrace of her compromised integrity. No matter what the adulterer does to negate her act, it will not go away. The wronged spouse will rightfully be enraged when he discovers what occurred. No money, no offering, and no bribe can undo the pain of a broken marriage covenant. God hates adultery, and yet we live in a culture that not only tolerates but often applauds sexual unfaithfulness. Despite what those around us may say or think and how they might trivialize our disdain for marital unfaithfulness, we must stand by what the Scripture declares. If you are the victim of a spouse's infidelity, you have been radically wronged. It is normal to be jealous and angry. However, God can both heal and repair your marriage. If you haven't already, get godly counsel and deal with the situation in honesty and humility.

My son, keep my words and treasure up my commandments with you; keep my commandments and live; keep my teaching as the apple of your eye;

Proverbs 7:1-2 ESV

The son is exhorted to keep the words and the commands of his wise father. Obedience to the father's instruction is literally a matter of life and death, and if the son follows the wisdom presented to him, he will enjoy an abundant life both now and eternally. The son is to guard the teaching he receives as one guards the pupil of her eye. The pupil is a very delicate and sensitive area of the body. In addition, it allows light to enter the eye. If the pupils aren't working properly, one is left with nothing but darkness. Just as the pupil must be zealously protected, so must the commands of the Lord. Do you guard your Bible reading time, or do you let the cares of this life keep you from reading the Scripture regularly? Determine to attentively read God's word, processing your thoughts through its truths today.

March

bind them on your fingers; write them on the tablet of your heart. Say to wisdom, "You are my sister," and call insight your intimate friend, to keep you from the forbidden woman, from the adulteress with her smooth words.

Proverbs 7:3-5 ESV

The son is called to memorize the commands of his father, even placing his father's teaching in visible places that he might always remember what he has learned. By continually putting wisdom into practice, the father's teaching becomes a part of the son's character and ends up written on his heart. "Sister" and "friend" are terms of endearment, and wisdom is to be viewed as a close family member or trusted companion. Again, the father's teaching will protect his son from sexual sin. Clearly, forbidden sex is mentioned often in the Proverbs. How do you view the commands of the Lord? Do you see them as a drag? Or do you cherish them like a best friend or a beloved family member? Our friends and family want nothing but the best for us, and the same is true for God's commands. Love the Scripture as much as you love those closest to you today.

> *For at the window of my house I have looked out through my lattice, and I have seen among the simple, I have perceived among the youths, a young man lacking sense,*

Proverbs 7:6-7 ESV

The father looks from the window of his house and observes members of his community. The wise learn from evaluating the attitudes and actions of others. While the father watched, he saw the simple, or those who would become easy prey for the wicked, and he noticed a specific young man who lacked sense. As the father considered those around him, he did so from his "window" or his worldview. He believed in a personal God whose nature is holy, and as the creator of all, demands a specific behavior from those he formed to inhabit his universe. The father was able to evaluate the actions of others through his worldview and pass wisdom on to his son. Do you believe in the existence of absolute right and wrong? If so, who or what determines what is proper behavior? These and other concepts shape our worldview and should be discussed with those we love.

passing along the street near her corner, taking the road to her house in the twilight, in the evening, at the time of night and darkness.

Proverbs 7:8-9 ESV

The wise father observed a young and naïve man who lacked sense. This young man carelessly and foolishly passed by the house of the adulteress, unaware of the danger she presented. He walked without thought, and he didn't cautiously consider where he was going. He just marched along mindlessly. Not only did he go into the wrong area of town, but he did so at the wrong time too! It was night, the time in which evil deeds hid under the cover of darkness. Like the simple man, we are fools as well if we choose to journey through life haphazardly, acting as if a carefree attitude is the best way to live. Instead, the wise woman thinks about where she is going, what she will do, and what the consequences of her decisions may be. An "anything goes" attitude toward life may sound like fun, but it simply isn't wise.

*And behold, the woman meets him,
dressed as a prostitute, wily of heart.
She is loud and wayward; her feet
do not stay at home; now in the street,
now in the market, and at every
corner she lies in wait.*

Proverbs 7:10-12 ESV

As the naïve man travels near the adulteress' home at night, out of nowhere, she suddenly appears. She actively seeks her victim out and knows exactly what to wear in order to seduce him. She intends to take advantage of him, seeking to gratify her own desires. In the end, she doesn't care about what happens to this man, as long as she gets what she wants. The adulteress is not satisfied with life and is continually on the prowl for something more attractive and exciting. She goes to the busiest places of town where the largest number of people will be found. Now, there's nothing wrong with enjoying people, activity, and busy city life, but this woman goes in order to devour. She intends to use others for selfish gain. Do you use people to get what you want? If so, ask God to change you today, teaching you to love in a way that glorifies him.

She seizes him and kisses him, and with bold face she says to him, "I had to offer sacrifices and today I have paid my vows; so now I have come out to meet you, to seek you eagerly, and I have found you.

Proverbs 7:13-15 ESV

The adulteress spots the naïve man and entices him. She is aggressive and won't allow him to leave without a fight. She is determined to overcome him and glories in the conquest of her victims. By grabbing and kissing him, she initiates her quest. She insists that she needs him for religious reasons, as she worships fertility gods. If rain ceased to fall, there would be no crops, and without crops there would be no harvest time. Those who worshipped fertility gods believed that by having sex they stimulated the gods to respond to their requirement for water, food, and fertility in general. The adulteress makes this simple man believe he is the only one who will satisfy. Those who initiate and pursue sexual sin are skilled in manipulation. When you cross paths with the one who flatters by insisting only you can meet his sexual needs, run the other way!

*I have spread my couch with coverings,
colored linens from Egyptian linen;
I have perfumed my bed with myrrh,
aloes, and cinnamon.*

Proverbs 7:16-17 ESV

The adulteress continues her aggressive pursuit of the simple man. Working to convince him that he is unique, she explains the "wonderful" things he will experience when he engages in sex with her. The bed is the finest, soft and arrayed in beautiful materials. And the scents are exhilarating. The young man could experience all that money has to offer if he simply steps through the door. If he denies her, he may never enjoy these delightful things again. How deceptive sin can be! It attempts to wear us down by thinking that God is withholding good from us. Just like the serpent deceived Eve into believing that God was keeping her from the best, darkness continues to speak today, pressing us to think we are being ripped off by holding fast to God's design. If you are feeling cheated at all because of obedience to Christ, resist Satan. He will flee from you.

Come, let us take our fill of love till morning; let us delight ourselves with love. For my husband is not at home; he has gone on a long journey; he took a bag of money with him; at full moon he will come home."

Proverbs 7:18-20 ESV

The adulteress attempts to persuade the naïve man to believe that the passionate sex she offers comes with no cost. Because her husband is out of town and won't return for a long time, she guarantees the young man that he has nothing to fear. But she should not be trusted! She's unfaithful to her marriage vow. Clearly, it would be stupid to believe she's telling the truth now. She is used to getting what she wants and will easily lie to manipulate the conscience of her victims. Of course she's not going to give up her life of luxury for the young fool. She only wants him for the night. What a portrait of sin's pattern! Just as Satan promised Eve that she would "not surely die," so the sin that easily entangles us attempts to assure us that we have nothing to fear. The wise recognize sin's ploy and resist its lure.

> With much seductive speech she
> persuades him; with her smooth talk
> she compels him. All at once he follows
> her, as an ox goes to the slaughter,
> or as a stag is caught fast

Proverbs 7:21-22 ESV

The adulteress is effective in her ploy. She nets the gullible man into her trap, and he follows her right to her bed. Her seductive words overcome any fear of the Lord he may hold. The father paints a shocking picture of sin's consequence and describes the man as an ox going to the slaughter. The ox is a strong animal, but because of its lack of sense, the creature will walk right into the place where its lifeblood will be drained from its body. Any sense or wisdom the man may have had was conquered by his desire for pleasure. There are times when we must simply choose to obey God rather than our feelings. If we need to be convinced of why something isn't for our best rather than trusting "because God said," we will eventually become ensnared by the same fate when our lusts override our logic.

till an arrow pierces its liver; as a bird rushes into a snare; he does not know that it will cost him his life. And now, O sons, listen to me, and be attentive to the words of my mouth.

Proverbs 7:23-24 ESV

The simple man enters the house of the adulteress and ends up in her bed. He gives in to her persistent pursuit, rejecting any wisdom he may have obtained over the years. An arrow in the liver promises sudden and certain demise. Like a dumb animal that doesn't realize the trap he is heading for leads to death, this man is oblivious to the fact that his sin will be his downfall. And so, the father makes his final appeal regarding sexual sin. Instead of listening to the manipulative and smooth words of the adulteress, the son must heed the wise and loving words of his father. How well do you listen to and apply the advice of the wise around you to your attitudes and actions? Which "voice" has the strongest influence over the decisions you make? Is it the opinion of the world or the wisdom of the word?

Let not your heart turn aside to her ways; do not stray into her paths, for many a victim has she laid low, and all her slain are a mighty throng. Her house is the way to Sheol, going down to the chambers of death.

Proverbs 7:25-27 ESV

Instead of wandering around aimlessly, walking where he shouldn't, the son is to stick to the path of wisdom. He must avoid the adulteress at all costs, as she will do whatever she can to take down whomever she can get. Even a mighty army is laid low by her manipulative techniques. The adulteress declares that by entering her house, the naïve man will experience passionate pleasure without consequence. But in reality, those who follow her walk to their death. It is important that we too be deliberate about what we think and what we do. If you were to honestly confess the area in which you are most tempted to sin, what would you say? How do you strategically avoid anything that might cause you to fall with respect to that particular sin? We can't drift near things that may entrap us and expect to stay on the path of wisdom at the same time.

Does not wisdom call? Does not understanding raise her voice? On the heights beside the way, at the crossroads she takes her stand; beside the gates in front of the town, at the entrance of the portals she cries aloud:

Proverbs 8:1-3 ESV

Wisdom calls to all who will listen, pleading with her audience to apply insight. She speaks on the heights, where everyone can see and hear, and by the way, where people choose which course they will take. She begs her audience at the crossroads to reject folly. She goes to the places where town matters are discussed and decisions are made. And she calls out for any who will listen to her voice before they embark along the way they've chosen. If we reject wisdom and make sinful choices in life, we have no one to blame but ourselves. Wisdom does not hide herself, even from the simple. Have you tuned out wisdom's plea or grown numb to her appeal? Is there an area where you know you aren't doing as you should, yet you rationalize and make excuses for your behavior? Listen to wisdom today, sparing yourself a life of regret.

"To you, O men, I call, and my cry is to the children of man. O simple ones, learn prudence; O fools, learn sense.

Proverbs 8:4-5 ESV

Wisdom cries out to humanity, including men and women, old and young, rich and poor. Wisdom is from above and makes herself available to everyone in need of objective knowledge and guidance. She desires both the simple and the foolish to learn and fix their hearts on sense. People come into life with a unique set of skills, talents and abilities. Some are more attractive than others, some more intelligent, and some are wired to get ahead in the world. But wisdom is available to all. Some will embrace her, and others will reject her. What about you? Will you determine to align your thinking and your behavior with what the Scripture teaches? Do you set off on the right course and then drift into self-indulgence and careless living? Ask the Holy Spirit to help you move forward without reservation as you purpose to gain and exercise wisdom today.

*Hear, for I will speak noble things,
and from my lips will come what is
right, for my mouth will utter truth;
wickedness is an abomination to my lips.*

Proverbs 8:6-7 ESV

The audience is to listen to the words of wisdom, which are correct and fair, as opposed to the speech of those who seek to lure the hearer into darkness. Suppose you could question someone about moral issues, ethical concerns, and things pertaining to truth, and know that every response to your inquiries is absolutely right and flawless. What would you ask such a person? What questions do you need answered? And what if the Scripture, the word of God, contains everything you need to know for life and godliness? Would you heed the Bible and obey what it teaches? In the end, who or what we believe to be the source of absolute truth drives what we think and do. Do you trust yourself, someone else, or God's word? Whom you listen to determines where you will go and eventually end up.

*All the words of my mouth are righteous;
there is nothing twisted or crooked in
them. They are all straight to him who
understands, and right to those who
find knowledge. Take my instruction
instead of silver, and knowledge
rather than choice gold.*

Proverbs 8:8-10 ESV

Wisdom speaks honestly, and because she seeks only the benefit of her hearer without any hint of self-service, her words contain no deceit. When a man understands the sincere intent of wisdom, he will seek her above what all others may suggest. Most people are driven by the love of money, but wisdom will not take a back seat to anything, even the finest life has to offer. The intelligent choose instruction above silver and gold. If one desires money or wealth more than wisdom, he may get the "stuff" he longs for but not the insight necessary to enjoy his prosperity. In the end, it is far better to have little and live uprightly than to pursue riches and all the fortunes of the word, yet remain a fool. If you had to choose between riches or wisdom, which would you pick? Are you living consistently with your choice?

for wisdom is better than jewels, and all that you may desire cannot compare with her. "I, wisdom, dwell with prudence, and I find knowledge and discretion. The fear of the Lord is hatred of evil. Pride and arrogance and the way of evil and perverted speech I hate.

Proverbs 8:11-12 ESV

Wisdom is to be desired above all things. The ability to navigate life rightly through life is dependent upon one's relationship to wisdom. The decisions we make right now will affect how our future unfolds. Wisdom teaches that the one who fears the Lord is the one who, like the Lord, hates evil. And evil is rooted in pride and arrogance, which refuse to submit to authority. In fact, an arrogant attitude leads to speech that seeks to exalt self against God and oppose his moral design. The phrase "question authority" was coined to protect against those who have historically abused power. But are God's people to question authority? Or should we just do as we are told? There's nothing wrong with questioning authority, as long as the questioning is done in light of God's word. In fact, we should search the Scripture continually to ensure that our behavior lines up with God's plan for human life.

I have counsel and sound wisdom; I have insight; I have strength. By me kings reign, and rulers decree what is just; by me princes rule, and nobles, all who govern justly.

Proverbs 8:14-16 ESV

Who would reject wisdom? She gives advice and insight, imparting great strength to those who heed her voice. Wisdom supplies her followers with the courage they need to put into practice all that she instructs. The qualities good leaders employ to successfully govern those they oversee are available to even the common person who embraces the instruction of wisdom. Those of honorable birth, such as kings and rulers and princes and nobles, are steered by wisdom. Those who are born again, having put their trust in Jesus and turned from a life of sin, are also of upright birth. With God as our Father, it has been said that though we remain lowly in the world, from heaven's perspective, we have royal blood in our veins. Are you making decisions consistent with your birthright? If you are a Christian today, you are a child of the King. Live in line with your calling.

I love those who love me, and those who seek me diligently find me. Riches and honor are with me, enduring wealth and righteousness.

Proverbs 8:17-18 ESV

Wisdom praises those who love her or desire to receive her instruction, and she will love them in return. There is a relationship between wisdom and her followers. Those who find her know and memorize her words. Those who have been rewired by God through faith in his Son will long for wisdom. And those who pursue wisdom will be blessed. Obedient living leads to a fruitful life. The wise are those who use their riches and honor for the benefit of others. Are you diligently seeking after wisdom? Do you spend time in God's word daily, pray for insight and direction, hear the Scripture preached in church, and turn to the righteous for counsel? If so, you will reap the benefit of being loved by wisdom. If not, you can change your course today. Above all, determine to listen to and apply wisdom's teaching. You can't afford not to!

My fruit is better than gold, even fine gold, and my yield than choice silver. I walk in the way of righteousness, in the paths of justice, granting an inheritance to those who love me, and filling their treasuries.

Proverbs 8:19-21 ESV

The benefits of living a wise life surpass even the luxuries of a rich life. Wisdom doesn't speak against wealth, and often riches are the benefit of living according to her words, but wisdom itself is always better than simple material blessing. Where is wisdom found? She is on the path of righteousness and justice. And she rewards those who love her. So what should we do to pursue and lay hold of wisdom? We must follow the way of the upright. If we cling to God's word and live according to his law and principles, we will walk alongside wisdom. Only the fool thinks she can travel with the scoffers, the sinners, and the wicked, and embrace wisdom at the same time. If you are leaning toward the path of disobedience, get back on the right track today. Love justice and mercy, and walk humbly before the Lord.

The Lord possessed me at the beginning of his work, the first of his acts of old. Ages ago I was set up, at the first, before the beginning of the earth.

Proverbs 8:22-23 ESV

Solomon's insight was from the Lord and has been revealed by God to all who would heed wisdom's counsel. The wise one listens to and obeys God's words. Before time began, God put things into motion according to his good and perfect plan. It is easy to forget that there is much more going on around us than meets the eye. Just because we can't see or hear or perceive something, doesn't mean it isn't there. Certain animals can hear sound frequencies that we can't sense or see colors unknown to us. Who can fathom how much exists beyond our detection? And yet, God chose to disclose to us the way of wisdom, though she be far above us. If you want to know her, humbly bow your heart before the Lord and admit your need for his direction. Allow wisdom to be your guide by following her wherever she wants you to go.

When there were no depths I was brought forth, when there were no springs abounding with water. Before the mountains had been shaped, before the hills I was brought forth, before he had made the earth with its fields, or the first of the dust of the world.

Proverbs 8:24-26 ESV

Wisdom existed before the universe was formed. Wisdom witnessed the Lord fashioning the earth from nothing, and she is ranked above all creation. The mountains are seen as strong, stable, and enduring the ages, yet wisdom stands above them. Before the dust of the earth existed—the very material man was formed from—wisdom was present. Clearly, wisdom takes priority over all the world has to offer. No matter how old or new an idea, wisdom was first. We can grow bored and look to something new or different for answers. We may jump on the latest bandwagons or attempt to revert to ancient practices in our quest to find meaning in life. If your heart is leaning toward a new fad or an old ritual, resist the desire to rest in anything other than God's wisdom. If God doesn't grow weary of the sunrise, the sunset, and other routine things in life, then neither should we.

When he established the heavens, I was there; when he drew a circle on the face of the deep, when he made firm the skies above, when he established the fountains of the deep,

---

Proverbs 8:27-28 ESV

Wisdom continues to list the things she witnessed before the world began. She was present when God created the universe. As God separated the water in the oceans from the water in the air, she watched. And when God established the water supply under the earth, wisdom was there. As we contemplate the creation and wisdom's presence alongside God from the beginning, we must admit we would be fools to reject her offer of guidance. We think and speak from limited knowledge and understanding, but when wisdom teaches first-hand, as she was present and in the front row while God brought all into existence. How simplistic we are to challenge the advice wisdom offers, somehow thinking we know better! In fact, we are unable to navigate through life without the wisdom of God. May the Lord move us to the place of silence before him today, where we are ready to hear and apply his word.

when he assigned to the sea its limit, so that the waters might not transgress his command, when he marked out the foundations of the earth, then I was beside him, like a master workman, and I was daily his delight, rejoicing before him always, rejoicing in his inhabited world and delighting in the children of man.

Proverbs 8:29-31 ESV

Wisdom watched as God put boundaries on the mighty sea, including the depths of the ocean and all they contain. Like the perfect paintbrush in an artist's hand, the Lord used wisdom as his tool when he created everything. Wisdom celebrated while the Lord worked. Beholding God's handiwork provides us all with reason after reason to rejoice. And wisdom has a special relationship with humanity: she is the one who brings God's truths to those who seek her. Our existence is totally dependent upon the earth, the sun, and even the universe continuing in the pattern that God mapped out. Were any of these complex systems to go awry, we would be brought back to the dust from which we came. Take a few minutes to praise God for all that he has created, giving special thanks for the way he designed you, fearfully and wonderfully made.

"And now, O sons, listen to me: blessed are those who keep my ways. Hear instruction and be wise, and do not neglect it. Blessed is the one who listens to me, watching daily at my gates, waiting beside my doors.

Proverbs 8:32-34 ESV

Wisdom strongly encourages her hearers to listen and keep her ways, as those who follow her advice will be blessed. In fact, the wise ones will not miss any opportunity to learn from her. How much effort and energy do you put into listening to wisdom's call? When you are in church, learning from your pastors, do you expect to hear wisdom's ways? Or do you tune the preacher out, thinking, "I already know this," or become distracted by the hairstyle of the woman near you, or allow your mind to drift to the day's lunch menu? Many interruptions can seek to keep us from actively watching and waiting to hear wisdom. We can carelessly tune out or even grow numb to her voice. The next time you attend church, wait for wisdom to speak directly to you. Wisdom has much to say to those ready to listen.

> *For whoever finds me finds life and obtains favor from the Lord, but he who fails to find me injures himself; all who hate me love death."*

Proverbs 8:35-36 ESV

Whoever finds wisdom finds eternal life and blessing from God. But to find wisdom doesn't mean to simply stumble upon her. Instead, it implies longing for and seeking after her. On the other hand, the one who does not hunt for wisdom, who is foolishly content to live according to what seems right in his own eyes, will suffer severely, both in this life and the life to come. God's laws and precepts are able to govern the affairs of men in a way consistent with his design. In heaven, there will be no more crying and pain, because all its inhabitants will live consistently with wisdom. It makes no sense to fear or reject God's will in your life now, because in heaven, where things are done his way, all will be perfectly right. If you desire heaven, where God's will is done, then live according his plan today.

April
6

Wisdom has built her house; she has hewn her seven pillars. She has slaughtered her beasts; she has mixed her wine; she has also set her table.

Proverbs 9:1-2 ESV

Wisdom brought her house into existence, including a roof supported by seven pillars, which meant her home was crafted with enough size to host a large number of guests. Wisdom prepared meat for a banquet and enhanced the taste of her wine. Though most didn't own a table, wisdom did, and she readied it for those who came to visit her. Wisdom doesn't sit around idly. She works to impart truth to those who would listen. Hard work is a by-product of wisdom. Those who want to follow her must prepare for what God calls them to. We can feel overwhelmed with commitments to work, family, and church and want to give up. But that's not wise! If we have much to do, we should be thankful. It is an honor to walk in the way of wisdom, leading busy and productive lives. Let's not shrink back from hard work; instead, let's rejoice in it.

She has sent out her young women to call from the highest places in the town, "Whoever is simple, let him turn in here!" To him who lacks sense she says, "Come, eat of my bread and drink of the wine I have mixed.

Proverbs 9:3-5 ESV

Wisdom prepares her home and banquet, and sends servants to invite guests to learn. Her attendants go to the city wall and cries out to any who would come, even those who lack sense. Those who respond will be nourished spiritually by her bread and wine. Will the hearer repent of doing life "his way" and acknowledge his need for wisdom, putting her insights into action and breaking bad habits? It can be hard to stop doing things the way we've always done them, but there's hope for the one who sees his need for a new start. Would you be willing to reset your thinking and actions if wisdom pointed out error in your life? Or are you set in your ways and too stubborn to break free of the poor decisions that entangle you? Join wisdom and begin life again with new passion and excitement today.

Leave your simple ways, and live, and walk in the way of insight." Whoever corrects a scoffer gets himself abuse, and he who reproves a wicked man incurs injury. Do not reprove a scoffer, or he will hate you; reprove a wise man, and he will love you.

Proverbs 9:6-8 ESV

Wisdom appeals to the simple, asking him to repent and find eternal life. Even the gullible can get on the right path if he responds to wisdom, putting her truths into practice. But a scoffer is unteachable. The mocker thinks he knows all and has no need for additional insight. In his anger, the scoffer will abuse the wise, speaking disdainfully about the one who attempts to correct him. The wicked man sees no error in his ways and believes he does nothing wrong. It's everyone else who needs help, not him. But, there is value in correcting the wise man. Because he fears God, he prizes direction and reproof. Do you consider yourself wise? If so, be characterized by taking criticism and correction well. The wise would never say, "I have done nothing wrong," but instead acknowledges room for growth, seeking to be aligned with God's standard for life.

Give instruction to a wise man, and he will be still wiser; teach a righteous man, and he will increase in learning. The fear of the Lord is the beginning of wisdom, and the knowledge of the Holy One is insight.

Proverbs 9:9-10 ESV

A wise man is teachable. He agrees he doesn't know everything and has room to improve. The basic principle of wisdom is the fear of the Lord. God is unlike any other being in the universe. Only God is qualified to determine which behaviors are upright and which are sinful. It is foolish for a human to speculate about acceptable behavior, because no man or woman's mind is unmarred by the effects of sin. We must turn to God in fear and in trust to discover the way of wisdom. The wise drink up the instruction of the Lord like a parched soul in a desert drinks from the fresh water of an oasis. He isn't ashamed of his need. When was the last time you were corrected, and how did you respond? Put any godly advice you have received into practice today. Don't let pride keep you from wisdom any longer.

For by me your days will be multiplied, and years will be added to your life. If you are wise, you are wise for yourself; if you scoff, you alone will bear it.

Proverbs 9:11-12 ESV

Wisdom benefits the wise and stands against the one who rejects her. Those who embrace wisdom will be blessed, and those who ignore her will suffer greatly. Few things in life impact a soul like a right response to wisdom . We are given one shot at this life, and our choices will make a difference now and eternally. Once God decides our time is up, there are no second chances. We will live forever with the consequences of what we did on earth. Not one thing or one experience this world can offer is worth more than living according to wisdom. What are you planning to get right in your life tomorrow or next week? Why wait? Instead of postponing, just do it now. How foolish we are to deliberately delay doing what we know will bless us in this life and eternally.

The woman Folly is loud; she is seductive and knows nothing. She sits at the door of her house; she takes a seat on the highest places of the town, calling to those who pass by, who are going straight on their way.

Proverbs 9:13-15 ESV

In contrast to wisdom stands folly, personified as Woman Wisdom and Woman Folly. Respectively, Folly lacks sense; although cunning, she knows nothing of morality. She appeals to the desire to do whatever "feels" right. She is unashamed to call out in public, although she's prepared nothing for her guests. She will provide the path of least resistance, and though idiotic, she will still attract followers. Folly does whatever she can to get the attention of those who pass by. Once she has their notice, she goes in for the kill. The fool doesn't intend to waste his life; he begins on the straight path, but after he fixes his eyes on folly, he can't seem to get her out of his head. Along your journey, there will be countless appeals for your attention. Don't entertain compromise for even a minute! Determine to fasten your heart to whatever is consistent with wisdom today.

"Whoever is simple, let him turn in here!" And to him who lacks sense she says, "Stolen water is sweet, and bread eaten in secret is pleasant." But he does not know that the dead are there, that her guests are in the depths of Sheol.

Proverbs 9:16-18 ESV

How odd! The foolish woman begs the simple, even the stupid man, to turn to her. Those who are unwise and lack judgment fall prey to folly. Wisdom presents a banquet before her followers, but folly offers stolen water and secret bread. Folly pushes the thrill of sin without mentioning the cost. Folly appeals again and again, some who are on the right path in life and seem to be wise will abandon what's right and join the senseless. But those who are truly wise will remain on the good path. Do you know people who seemed to "get it," only later to return to the ways of the world? If you are tempted to steer from the right way today and spend some time in the house of the fool, resist the urge. Reject the momentary pleasure of disobedience for the reward of righteousness.

The proverbs of Solomon. A wise son makes a glad father, but a foolish son is a sorrow to his mother. Treasures gained by wickedness do not profit, but righteousness delivers from death.

Proverbs 10:1-2 ESV

One must listen to and apply teaching from those who have gone before, and the son who lives according to wisdom will accept the instruction of his father and his mother. The foolish son brings grief to his family. He hurts not only those closest to him, but the community at large. None benefit from the actions of the unwise son. Although money can buy a more comfortable life, a bank account will not help in the life to come. Not one person will be able to buy her way out of hell. In fact, we all will be judged based on how we used the financial resources God has graced us with. And so, as the righteous use their wealth to benefit others, they will be blessed eternally for acting appropriately with their money. Are you generous with what God has given you, or are you tight-fisted with your wallet?

The Lord does not let the righteous go hungry, but he thwarts the craving of the wicked. A slack hand causes poverty, but the hand of the diligent makes rich.

Proverbs 10:3-4 ESV

God sees to it that his people will be provided for. The hunger Solomon speaks of represents the appetites and desires of life. The deepest longings are satisfied in the one who has made peace with God through Jesus. His soul is whole, well and reconciled to the Creator. But the wicked man, no matter how much he attains in this life, will never be genuinely content. Because he chases after things that cannot fill the God-shaped hole in his heart, he simply cannot be at ease. Nevertheless, financial lack often results from laziness. Those who work hard are blessed with the things they need. Through self-discipline and persistence, the determined acquire things of genuine value in life. Do you consider yourself a hard worker? What about in your church? Are you making an impact for the Lord and his kingdom? God blesses those who are diligent.

He who gathers in summer is a prudent son, but he who sleeps in harvest is a son who brings shame. Blessings are on the head of the righteous, but the mouth of the wicked conceals violence.

Proverbs 10:5-6 ESV

A hardworking and disciplined son brings honor to his parents. But the son who is unmoved by his surroundings, making little to no effort to grab the opportunity for gain presented to him, is an embarrassment. The blessing of a son should cause joy in the hearts of his parents, but the parents of the slothful son are clothed in shame. The one who is righteous is spoken well of and blessed by others as he is encouraged and prayed for. Violence is spoken of by the wicked man, and his dark and selfish words will come back to haunt him. How do you feel about hard work? Do you do the minimum to get by, or do you labor diligently, doing all for Jesus? You are called to give your very best effort for as long as you can. You never know when your opportunity will be gone.

The memory of the righteous is a blessing, but the name of the wicked will rot. The wise of heart will receive commandments, but a babbling fool will come to ruin. Whoever walks in integrity walks securely, but he who makes his ways crooked will be found out.

Proverbs 10:7-9 ESV

The name of the righteous person brings blessing to the hearer, but the memory of the wicked is soon blotted out, rotting like worm-eaten wood. The wise humbly recognize their need for and receive instruction, while the fool, who knows it all, rambles on and on about his opinions. The one on the path of righteousness travels through life in spiritual safety. But the fruit of his actions will expose the one who deviates from truth. Have you ever been around a person who won't stop talking long enough to listen to reason? Even when she is quiet, she hears nothing but her own voice. This is the person who will come to ruin. Don't be the one who always has to be right. Accept good and godly advice, agreeing that you still have more to learn. Display your wisdom through a willingness to be instructed.

*Whoever winks the eye causes trouble,
and a babbling fool will come to ruin.
The mouth of the righteous is a fountain
of life, but the mouth of the wicked
conceals violence. Hatred stirs up strife,
but love covers all offenses.*

Proverbs 10:10-12 ESV

The troublemaker causes strife in her community, and the one who won't stop talking long enough to hear and receive instruction is destined for disaster. The words that come from the righteous bring life, while the speech of the wicked is self-serving, creating hostility, though its intentions are veiled. Water represents life, and those who are godly speak words that bring healing and life to others, whether through encouragement or correction. In this life, miscommunication and even sinful words will occur, but the one who truly loves will protect and defend others, avoiding slander and gossip, and doing whatever she can to help her friends be reconciled to God. The one who loves never gives up, even on her enemies. Have you "thrown in the towel" on a friend or family member? Maybe it's time to begin to pray for her again, begging the Lord to reconcile your relationship with her and her relationship with God.

On the lips of him who has understanding, wisdom is found, but a rod is for the back of him who lacks sense. The wise lay up knowledge, but the mouth of a fool brings ruin near.

Proverbs 10:13-14 ESV

The wise person speaks insightful words because God has worked his wisdom into her heart as she applied the insight given to her. On the other hand, the one without this sense requires force to motivate her right behavior. Whether it be from a loving parent or even our God, discipline gets us on the right path. The wise store up the knowledge they receive, and are prepared to counter the fools, who lacks wisdom and may spout off at any time, destroying others with their thoughtless speech. If we are God's children, we choose to line up our thinking and actions under his law and principles. But if his children, go against wisdom, he will do what it takes to correct us. If you are disobedient in any area of life as a Christian, repent. Ask God to forgive you, and stop the sin today before the corrective rod comes out.

A rich man's wealth is his strong city;
the poverty of the poor is their ruin.
The wage of the righteous leads to life,
the gain of the wicked to sin.

Proverbs 10:15-16 ESV

There are positive and negative aspects of wealth. The one who is rich risks the temptation to put her trust in money. In the end, her security is only imaginary. On the day she dies, her riches won't benefit her at all in the judgment. In fact, they will only provide additional means for evaluating whether she acted wisely with the abundance God blessed her with. Poverty can cause great terror in a soul and potentially leave one in a state of utter panic. Those who are righteous know how to manage wealth in a way that honors the Lord. God graces those whom he has made righteous with eternal life, while the earnings of the wicked result in death. No matter how large your house, retirement plan, or bank account, you will one day stand empty-handed before the Lord. Are you using your wealth to lay up an eternal reward?

Whoever heeds instruction is on the path to life, but he who rejects reproof leads others astray. The one who conceals hatred has lying lips, and whoever utters slander is a fool.

Proverbs 10:17-18 ESV

The wise are exhorted to memorize the instruction they've been given, and this charge includes putting it into practice. We see this principle repeatedly in the Proverbs. Those who have access to, listen to, and even recite wisdom without living out her counsel may know much, but they understand little. Those who reject wisdom are accountable for the others they bring down to death with them. The wicked practice deceit and slander, motivated by hatred. Have you run across the woman who appears to be gracious and upright, yet habitually reveals dirt about others who have "wronged" her? Does she portray herself as the continual victim? Underneath this speech lies a heart of hatred. If you know this woman, or worse, if you are this woman, repent today. Confess your bitterness, asking God to free you from bondage to darkness. You may be misleading others, but you aren't deceiving the Lord.

When words are many, transgression is not lacking, but whoever restrains his lips is prudent. The tongue of the righteous is choice silver; the heart of the wicked is of little worth. The lips of the righteous feed many, but fools die for lack of sense.

Proverbs 10:19-21 ESV

The more words, the greater the opportunity for sin. Therefore, the one who restrains herself from talking too much is wise. In fact, when the wise speak, they are thoughtful and use care rather than spewing out whatever comes to mind. The wise person realizes the power of her words, and keeps a guard upon her tongue. When the righteous speak, their words are valuable and free from worthless components. But the wicked person's speech is steeped in evil because of the darkness she holds in her heart. The words of the righteous bring life to those who hear, but those who listen to the fool end up dying, the fool's speech is empty and devoid of anything life-giving. What kinds of words come from your mouth? Do they feed and encourage the hearers, or do they break down and dishearten others? How would your husband respond to the same question if he had to answer about you?

The blessing of the Lord makes rich, and he adds no sorrow with it. Doing wrong is like a joke to a fool, but wisdom is pleasure to a man of understanding.

Proverbs 10:22-23 ESV

God provides wealth, and though some may labor strenuously, if the Lord does not chose to financially bless, the effort is in vain. The riches that come from the Lord aren't followed by painful consequences, but enjoyed by a heart full of gratitude. The fool is pleased when he engages in wrongful and destructive behavior. Though jokes and pranks can be amusing, the fool crosses the boundary of common decency and will easily break the law for a good laugh. The same things don't entertain those who follow the Lord. Instead, the wise person is satisfied by right and productive deeds. As you journey along the path of wisdom, you will discover that many of the things the world finds entertaining aren't comical to you. But that doesn't mean the upright have no sense of humor. Instead, Christians should be the most joyful people on the planet. When was the last time you laughed, and at what?

What the wicked dreads will come upon him, but the desire of the righteous will be granted. When the tempest passes, the wicked is no more, but the righteous is established forever. Like vinegar to the teeth and smoke to the eyes, so is the sluggard to those who send him.

Proverbs 10:24-26 ESV

Even the wicked man has a conscience, and deep in his soul he knows he will reap the consequences of his evil behavior. The righteous person will ultimately see what he longs for: God's kingdom established. In time, the wicked will be swept away in God's judgment, but the righteous will live with the Lord forever. Unlike good wine, which was diluted for refreshment, vinegar eats away at the enamel of the teeth, hurting the one who drinks it. When preparing a fire for cooking, if smoke enters the eyes, it burns. In the same way, the sluggard brings disappointment, pain, and even harm to the one who entrusted her with a task. When you are asked to do something, do you faithfully accomplish what you've been assigned, or do you fail to deliver? The lazy person is not only useless, but harmful as well. Resist any desire to be unfaithful to what's expected of you today.

The fear of the Lord prolongs life, but the years of the wicked will be short. The hope of the righteous brings joy, but the expectation of the wicked will perish.

Proverbs 10:27-28 ESV

The righteous fear the Lord. They have a healthy respect for God and his power to give and take life. The wicked don't share the same fear of God. They refuse to acknowledge his authority and rule over creation, and they feel qualified to set their own standard of right and wrong behavior. Even if the wicked live over a hundred years, their "life" is a token compared to the eternal life promised to the righteous. Those who fear and obey the Lord eagerly await the coming day when everything will be made just right. This will be a time of great joy and continual rejoicing. If you belong to God, no matter how difficult this life may feel, this is the worst it will ever be for you. And if you haven't turned to God through Christ in repentance and faith, your life on earth is the best you will ever get.

The way of the Lord is a stronghold to the blameless, but destruction to evildoers. The righteous will never be removed, but the wicked will not dwell in the land.

Proverbs 10:29-30 ESV

The wellbeing of those who are righteous and the devastation of those who are wicked are a direct result of the way of the Lord. God will reward those who have trusted and turned to him with eternal life. At the same time, he promises to visit judgment upon those who reject his terms of salvation. It is only by following the wisdom of the Lord that a soul can be truly secure. The day is coming when each person will stand before God to give an account of whether she lived according to God's design or did things her own way. All who fail to meet God's standard of perfection will be cut off from his grace forever. But those who confess their sin, place their trust in Christ, and turn to God in repentance are made righteous. If you are saved, you are in the most secure place in the universe. Nothing can harm you spiritually.

The mouth of the righteous brings forth wisdom, but the perverse tongue will be cut off. The lips of the righteous know what is acceptable, but the mouth of the wicked, what is perverse.

Proverbs 10:31-32 ESV

The words of the righteous are consistent with the revelation of God and bring life to those who hear them. The wicked challenge the Lord and his design for humanity. They arrogantly think they know more than God and if they were in charge they would do things differently, not realizing that their sense of goodness, justice, and love has been given to them from the Lord. The condition of the soul is revealed by speech. Those who are right with God exercise discretion, knowing what is both beneficial to others and consistent with truth. The wicked seek to persuade people to reject God's authority over their lives. Do you have friends or family members who push you to doubt the Lord and his wisdom? In times of discouragement, are you the one who fosters unbelief in others? Listen to those who speak truth in love, and make sure you think before you talk.

A false balance is an abomination to the Lord, but a just weight is his delight. When pride comes, then comes disgrace, but with the humble is wisdom.

Proverbs 11:1-2 ESV

The balance is a measuring device with two plates, one on each side, for comparison. A fixed amount of weight is put in one plate, and an item in the other. In this way, fair amounts of a traded good were determined. Merchants carried weights of standard measure, their accuracy was assumed. The dishonest trader used a weight that was too light when selling and one that was too heavy when buying. That way, she could sell less than what was agreed to and buy more than her share for the price. In God's eyes, dishonest people not only steal from the community, but deny him as well. The Lord will humble the one who has an inflated view of self. Wisdom generates a realistic outlook on personal skills, talents, and abilities. Remember that ripping one another off is repulsive to God. Be completely honest in all of your transactions today.

The integrity of the upright guides them, but the crookedness of the treacherous destroys them. Riches do not profit in the day of wrath, but righteousness delivers from death. The righteousness of the blameless keeps his way straight, but the wicked falls by his own wickedness.

Proverbs 11:3-5 ESV

Those who follow the Lord will be safely led to their eternal home, even though they will experience difficulties in this life. The unrighteous face a bitter end, filled with violence and devastation. Many spend their lives seeking to amass a financial fortune, but in death it will profit nothing. Not one will buy her way out of the judgment or take the world's goods with her into the life to come. Our only hope of standing on the last day is rooted in our response to the gospel of God. The journey of the righteous is free from stumbling blocks, while the way of the wicked is loaded with spiritual obstacles that lead to his ultimate demise. The Proverbs address the topic of money often. Clearly, finances are an important factor in the daily decisions we make. What is your attitude toward money? Are you using your wealth to build God's kingdom, or your own?

The righteousness of the upright delivers them, but the treacherous are taken captive by their lust. When the wicked dies, his hope will perish, and the expectation of wealth perishes too. The righteous is delivered from trouble, and the wicked walks into it instead.

Proverbs 11:6-8 ESV

Those who are upright will be delivered from death, while the wicked are ensnared by the very things they desire. When the wicked man dies, there is nothing left for him. He is cut off from the presence of God and his kindness. Any ability he had to better his situation while on earth is gone. The Lord will ultimately protect the righteous from trouble, but the wicked don't share in this promise from God. Although no one is blameless, those who see their need for forgiveness put their trust in the provision of Christ, turn to God, and are willing to walk along the path of wisdom will be credited with the righteousness of Jesus and will spend eternity in heaven. After life comes to an end, there is nothing good for those without Jesus. Death truly changes everything. What on earth is keeping you from responding to God today?

With his mouth the godless man would destroy his neighbor, but by knowledge the righteous are delivered. When it goes well with the righteous, the city rejoices, and when the wicked perish there are shouts of gladness. By the blessing of the upright a city is exalted, but by the mouth of the wicked it is overthrown.

Proverbs 11:9-11 ESV

The ungodly use gossip to destroy those around them. They pretend friendship to gain access to the heart of their neighbors, only to turn around and use revealed personal information to bring their "friends" down. The wise recognize the godless and resist their manipulative ways. The righteous avoid intimacy with those who have the "dirt" on other members of the community. The godly rejoice when the enemies of the Lord fall, but the wicked create wars among friends. Relationships built by laboring together for the Lord can be demolished by the slander of the wicked. Have you ever crossed paths with the woman who wants to let you in on problems with fellow believers? How foolish to fight with our teammates. We should battle against the enemies of our God and not one another. Exercise wisdom and walk away from negative talk about any of God's people today.

Whoever belittles his neighbor lacks sense,
but a man of understanding remains
silent. Whoever goes about slandering
reveals secrets, but he who is trustworthy
in spirit keeps a thing covered.

Proverbs 11:12-13 ESV

Though we may see faults in our neighbors, as humans, they bear the image of God, and are therefore valuable to him. It is foolish then to express disdain toward your neighbors, as they are of great worth to the Lord. The one who is wise controls her tongue, refraining from revealing everything she knows. The woman of understanding is not fueled by hate or vengeance, but loves those around her, keeping the confidence of her friends. The one who makes public the private conversations between so-called friends destroys the community by creating trouble. Jealousy, revenge, financial gain, or a fondness for trouble drives the wicked woman to sever relationships. When you are privy to information about another, do you leak it out or do you remain quiet? How would you feel if your innermost secrets and struggles became public knowledge? Do right by protecting the reputation of others today.

Where there is no guidance, a people falls, but in an abundance of counselors there is safety. Whoever puts up security for a stranger will surely suffer harm, but he who hates striking hands in pledge is secure.

Proverbs 11:14-15 ESV

If a community or even an individual hopes for success, it is wise to seek after good counsel before making decisions. When leading others, we should humbly resist any desire to rule independently of advice. It's also important to ask for wisdom before entering into financial contracts, including the desire to cosign for another. To whom do you go for godly counsel? Do you have a couple of friends who love God and his word and will direct you to his laws and principles for insight? Or do you desire to seem the wise one and end up foolishly neglecting God's gift of solid counsel? What about in your marriage? Do you consult your husband before making decisions for your household and your kids? Or are you calling the shots on your own? We set ourselves up for error and regret when we fail to get the input of others.

A gracious woman gets honor, and violent men get riches. A man who is kind benefits himself, but a cruel man hurts himself. The wicked earns deceptive wages, but one who sows righteousness gets a sure reward.

Proverbs 11:16-18 ESV

A single woman who is admired is of more worth than many men with wealth. A woman displaying inner beauty is superior to those who ruthlessly pursue money, as their wickedness keeps them from enjoying their riches. A kind man sacrifices his time and resources for the good of others, and he is blessed. The one who is selfish and cruel will not prosper in the end. Ultimately, the wicked will suffer, while the righteous will be rewarded. The noble in character are pleasing to the Lord. God highly values the woman who possesses a quiet and gentle spirit. This doesn't mean that she can't speak, but she is marked by inward satisfaction, knowing that God has everything under control. Do others see you as a woman satisfied with what she has? If not, ask him to help you to refrain from craving more and be content today.

Whoever is steadfast in righteousness will live, but he who pursues evil will die. Those of crooked heart are an abomination to the Lord, but those of blameless ways are his delight. Be assured, an evil person will not go unpunished, but the offspring of the righteous will be delivered.

Proverbs 11:19-21 ESV

The righteous will experience eternal life, while the wicked, who chase down opportunities to fulfill self-seeking desires, will be separated from God now and forever. God dwells with those whose hearts are blameless. Oh, how we all need his mercy and grace to be found guiltless before the Lord. He promises that those who live outside of his design for human behavior will experience wrath, but his favor is upon those who have cast themselves upon Jesus, trusting in his work upon the cross. Sadly, many fail to see their need for redemption. They honestly believe that if they end up before God's throne, they will be deemed "good" and granted access into heaven based on their works. Pray that God would reveal to you how short you fall when it comes to his standard of righteousness. Yet, if you are in Christ today, God sees you as spotless. What a reason for joy!

Like a gold ring in a pig's snout is a beautiful woman without discretion. The desire of the righteous ends only in good; the expectation of the wicked in wrath.

Proverbs 11:22-23 ESV

In the ancient Near East, women wore nose rings as accessories. The nose ring tastefully accentuated beauty and was a symbol of wealth. Pigs, on the other hand, were unclean animals, and those who followed the Lord were forbidden from consuming them as food. Pigs lived in the mud and ate just about anything to excess. How foolish to take a beautiful accessory and put it in the pig's nose, which would be saturated with dirt and dung. Worse is the beautiful woman who fails to use sound judgment in her dress and behavior. This woman goes against God's plan for her sexuality, and by flaunting herself she becomes unattractive and ugly before the Lord. Avoid focusing merely on your external appearance, and instead invest in inward beauty. Don't unwisely expose your body to gain the attention of others. True daughters of the King employ modesty and dignity in their appearance, actions, and attitudes.

One gives freely, yet grows all the richer; another withholds what he should give, and only suffers want. Whoever brings blessing will be enriched, and one who waters will himself be watered. The people curse him who holds back grain, but a blessing is on the head of him who sells it.

Proverbs 11:24-26 ESV

The one who graciously distributes her resources, generously investing in the needs of others, ends up with more than she originally gave. The one who is stingy ends up deprived of even basic resources. A satisfied life is the reward of those who provide for others, and abundant blessing is showered upon those who provide for the poor. The community looks down on the one who hoards life's necessities, but happy is the one who makes her resources available to those around her. The Lord gives good gifts to all, and he expects his kids to be characterized by generosity as a result. Thinking about your recent bank transactions, would you say you are a generous person? If you struggle financially, might you be suffering the consequences of stinginess? Even if you don't have much, give to those less fortunate than you. God will reward your kindness, both in this life and the life to come.

Whoever diligently seeks good seeks favor, but evil comes to him who searches for it. Whoever trusts in his riches will fall, but the righteous will flourish like a green leaf.

Proverbs 11:27-28 ESV

From a desire to please the Lord, the wise work hard for the welfare of others, and they receive the blessing of God. Those who enjoy seeing their neighbors suffer harm will find that the distress they want for others will come back to them. The one who protects his finances, neglecting to help the poor, will have nothing stored up for himself in the end, but those who are generous will prosper. People recognize that those who look out for others end up doing well themselves, while the ones who are mean-spirited end up suffering loss. This principle isn't the result of an impersonal force; it exists because God is directly involved in the affairs of men. All humans bear the image of God, so when we do good to others, we bless the Lord. And when we seek to harm others, we grieve the Lord. God is extremely interested in how we treat people.

Whoever troubles his own household will inherit the wind, and the fool will be servant to the wise of heart. The fruit of the righteous is a tree of life, and whoever captures souls is wise. If the righteous is repaid on earth, how much more the wicked and the sinner!

Proverbs 11:29-31 ESV

The person who ruins the relationships in her own household, bringing trouble upon her family and extended family, will be left with nothing. This foolish woman ends up rejected by her own and must serve another to survive. In contrast, the wisdom of the righteous woman is attractive to others, providing truth and love to those who come into contact with her. Since God disciplines his own children, teaching and training them to live in line with his laws and principles, surely he will punish those who reject him and are outside of his care all together. Though it may appear that the wicked prosper in this life, their judgment is certain. How have your words and actions impacted others over the last few days? Do you bring healing and life, or do you damage and dishearten those around you? Would the people closest to you say you typically build others up or tear them down?

Whoever loves discipline loves knowledge, but he who hates reproof is stupid. A good man obtains favor from the Lord, but a man of evil devices he condemns. No one is established by wickedness, but the root of the righteous will never be moved.

Proverbs 12:1-3 ESV

The person who embraces teaching and training is wise. The one who turns from correction is dumb. In her ignorance, she behaves more like an animal than a human, going with whatever "feels" right or whatever her sinful nature "wants" to do, rather than God's desire. God blesses the one who seeks to live according to his standards, and he judges those who reject his laws. The one who is right with the Lord will never be shaken. She will bear fruit, and her fruit will remain. How do you respond to the Lord's correction? When you learn that your behavior is inconsistent with his design, do you align your attitudes and actions with his will? Are you rationalizing and making excuses for a particular area of sin? The wise woman admits that she needs help, and when her errors are revealed, she leans on Jesus, asking him to enable her to get things right.

An excellent wife is the crown of her husband, but she who brings shame is like rottenness in his bones. The thoughts of the righteous are just; the counsels of the wicked are deceitful.

Proverbs 12:4-5 ESV

Two types of wives are contrasted: excellent and rotten. In both cases, the husband's reputation is affected by his wife's behavior. The God-fearing wife is like a crown upon a man's head. She is faithful, hardworking, and manages her home with order, kindness, and generosity. She does what she can to enable her husband to serve the Lord. The ungodly wife is like a hidden source of decay. She is immoral, argumentative, and self-seeking. She makes life hard for her husband in the home and the community. Those who are right with God desire fairness, while the enemies of the Lord scheme to get whatever they can for themselves. If you are married, does God see you as an excellent wife? Do you encourage your husband? Or do you view yourself as superior to him, wishing he would get his act together? God expects wives to love their husbands, and he holds them accountable to do so.

The words of the wicked lie in wait for blood, but the mouth of the upright delivers them. The wicked are overthrown and are no more, but the house of the righteous will stand.

Proverbs 12:6-7 ESV

Those who are wicked use their speech to entrap and harm. But those who are upright communicate words of salvation, undoing the destructive messages of the ungodly. In the end, God ensures that his words, taught to a dying world, will bear fruit. God is aware of all that takes place in the universe. Those who desire to use their words to harm others will end up harmed themselves. The followers of the Lord, who hear the gospel, rightly respond to it, and put it into practice, will not be shaken, even in the final judgment. The Lord frowns upon those who seek to damage the reputation of others by using gossip or slander. How do you speak about your enemies? Do you tear them down before others, or do you bless them and speak kindly about them instead? God is opposed to those who desire to see the downfall of others, especially fellow believers.

A man is commended according to his good sense, but one of twisted mind is despised. Better to be lowly and have a servant than to play the great man and lack bread. Whoever is righteous has regard for the life of his beast, but the mercy of the wicked is cruel.

Proverbs 12:8-10 ESV

Wise decisions bring praise from the community, but the one who acts upon selfish impulses and desires, though highly esteemed by others for a season, will eventually be seen as worthless. A godly person chooses to live comfortably without need for recognition. The fool will show off her resources in an attempt to gain acceptance, even though she often actually has nothing to display. It is never smart to pretend to be something you aren't, physically or spiritually. The righteous person is compassionate, extending mercy to even her animals. The heartless allow others to suffer for personal gain. It is odd that people try so hard to impress each other. How miserable we must appear before God as we struggle and strive to look good in the eyes of man. May we be driven by a desire to be upright before the Lord today, and trust him with what others think of us.

Whoever works his land will have plenty of bread, but he who follows worthless pursuits lacks sense. Whoever is wicked covets the spoil of evildoers, but the root of the righteous bears fruit.

Proverbs 12:11-13 ESV

The diligent worker will have enough to satisfy her hunger, while the one who chases after worthless endeavors and "get rich quick" schemes will not prosper. Though God often allows the righteous to suffer, the Proverbs teach that hard labor is rewarded. The proven character of a righteous person yields stability, protection, and provision. The wicked long to take shortcuts and look for easy ways to wealth and leisure. Be wary of entangling yourself in any business venture that preys upon friends and family for monetary gain, promising quick cash with little to no effort. When a financial situation seems too good to be true, it usually is. Use caution and steer away from so-called opportunities to get to the top fast. God smiles upon those who humbly use the talents he has graced them with to earn a legitimate living, while keeping themselves free from the love of money.

An evil man is ensnared by the transgression of his lips, but the righteous escapes from trouble. From the fruit of his mouth a man is satisfied with good, and the work of a man's hand comes back to him. The way of a fool is right in his own eyes, but a wise man listens to advice.

Proverbs 12:13-15 ESV

The wicked attempt to destroy the righteous by speaking against them. The Lord will allow the tables to turn, and the evil person will be entrapped by the very harm she intended for the upright. The righteous person lives well within her community. She exhibits the fruit of the Spirit because her inner person has been born again, and she has genuine love for all people. The Lord will reward her godly decisions. Only the fool thinks she has no need for correction. The one who is wise admits that she has and will continue to make mistakes. She listens to the advice of others without being defensive or stubborn. Have you met the woman who insists she has done nothing but right, and there is no way she could improve upon her actions? Are you that woman? If so, ask a godly person for counsel, putting an end to your foolishness today.

The vexation of a fool is known at once, but the prudent ignores an insult. Whoever speaks the truth gives honest evidence, but a false witness utters deceit. There is one whose rash words are like sword thrusts, but the tongue of the wise brings healing.

Proverbs 12:16-18 ESV

The foolish woman fails to control her emotions. When she's been wronged, she lets everyone know. She loves the fight and doesn't seek to resolve differences with others. The one who is wise holds her tongue when accused and readily forgives those who have offended her. Her composure vindicates her character. The honest witness tells the entire truth in court, and doesn't add to or leave out facts in an attempt to damage others. Just as a sword can harm or kill, so can the words of the woman who speaks against another. The wise woman seeks restoration and reconciliation in relationships, desiring the glory of God over personal vindication. When you have been misunderstood, are you passionate about making sure your public image is protected? When those who love God wrestle with one another regarding who was right and wrong, the world watches and laughs. Learn to truly let it go for the sake of the gospel.

Truthful lips endure forever, but a lying tongue is but for a moment. Deceit is in the heart of those who devise evil, but those who plan peace have joy. No ill befalls the righteous, but the wicked are filled with trouble.

Proverbs 12:19-21 ESV

Those who speak truth uphold laws and principles established by God. But lies are rejected by the Lord and will not endure the test of time. The wicked use deceit to forward their plans. They desire to hurt others and craftily communicate, creating division. Those who long for reconciliation will experience the joy of the Lord. In the end, God will vindicate the one who has done things his way. When we have been hurt, we often want to bring pain upon those who have caused our suffering. The hearts of some become dark, and they refuse to see God's hand in their trials. But what if God reveals you were not treated unfairly in the situation you are angry about? Just because you feel you have been wronged doesn't mean you have actually been wronged. If you are at odds with another, do whatever you can to remedy that today. Be at peace with everyone.

Lying lips are an abomination to the Lord, but those who act faithfully are his delight. A prudent man conceals knowledge, but the heart of fools proclaims folly.

Proverbs 12:22-23 ESV

God is truth, and he cannot tolerate those who lie. The trustworthy are pleasing in his sight. When they interact with others, they can be counted on to be honest. In our communication, if we cause another to believe something other than the truth, we have lied. At the same time, the wise must often, for the sake of love, refrain from divulging all that she knows. It isn't always helpful to reveal everything, and if our disclosure of information will harm another, then it's often best to remain silent. The fool, on the other hand, feels the need to let everyone know when she's been wronged. The Lord is watching all that goes on among his people. He sees the one who moves from person to person, tearing down others in an attempt to build herself up. Just as a parent will deal with disobedience in her children, God will discipline those who cause harm with their words.

The hand of the diligent will rule, while the slothful will be put to forced labor. Anxiety in a man's heart weighs him down, but a good word makes him glad.

Proverbs 12:24-25 ESV

Those who work hard will eventually rise up to positions of leadership. But the woman who is not self-motivated, failing to manage her time and energy well, will end up forced to work for another. Fear leads to anxiety, and anxiety creates an unnecessary burden on the soul, which can lead to depression and a desire to quit trying. But the encouraging word of a friend brings hope and healing to the restless heart. Jesus taught his disciples about the crippling effects of anxiety. He reminded them that if they had food and clothing they were to be content, as he promised to never leave or forsake them. Do you help others to be sensible? Or do you cause them to feel weighed down and even hopeless? If you are married, do you encourage your husband, or does he hear that he's not doing enough to make you happy?

One who is righteous is a guide to his neighbor, but the way of the wicked leads them astray. Whoever is slothful will not roast his game, but the diligent man will get precious wealth. In the path of righteousness is life, and in its pathway there is no death.

Proverbs 12:26-28 ESV

The righteous person carefully considers which women she will call her true friends. She looks for those who can both give her wisdom and keep her confident. But the wicked will confide in just about anyone. They are misguided and aren't looking for sound advice. The lazy person doesn't follow through on what she starts and ends up with nothing to enjoy. The one who begins and finishes well will be rewarded. Those whom God has made righteous will never experience separation from him in this life or in the life to come. The Lord will never abandon those who have placed their trust in his Son, Jesus Christ. Although we will all one day leave the physical bodies we inhabit, for those who are righteous, life will not only continue but flourish. If you have put off getting things right with God, don't resist his Spirit any longer. Choose life today.

A wise son hears his father's instruction, but a scoffer does not listen to rebuke. From the fruit of his mouth a man eats what is good, but the desire of the treacherous is for violence.

Proverbs 13:1-2 ESV

The Proverbs again exhort the wise son to listen to the instruction of his parents. Unlike the mocker or scoffer, who doesn't receive correction when he sins, the wise son embraces the path of obedience. The unwise person has no desire to profit from sound advice. But the son who ingests the teaching of his parents is like a man who eats what is good, experiencing blessing. The unfaithful man, who cannot be trusted, thirsts for violence. He doesn't use his words to help others, but to inflict harm. How odd to consider that there have always been people who honestly desire to bring pain to others using cruel, mean, and even hateful words. Watch out for the one who turns to vehicles such as prayer requests and accountability to demolish the reputation of others. God is not pleased when we use speech to hurt those who have been created in his image.

Whoever guards his mouth preserves his life; he who opens wide his lips comes to ruin. The soul of the sluggard craves and gets nothing, while the soul of the diligent is richly supplied.

Proverbs 13:3-4 ESV

When one wisely uses her words, it can actually protect her life. But the woman who is not cautious with her words will come to ruin. There is great wisdom in rejecting the desire to say everything that crosses our minds. We must learn to exercise self-control when it comes to our speech. Just as the one who speaks carelessly brings harm to the community, so does the one who fails to work. The sluggard expects to be provided for and is a drain on others. The woman who diligently seeks what is good will be rewarded, and as she pursues the Lord, he himself will satisfy her longings. Sometimes it seems like the irresponsible among us prosper, while the hardworking struggle. But we should never grow weary of doing what's right. God sees all, and he will reward his people as they press on by faith and not by sight.

The righteous hates falsehood, but the wicked brings shame and disgrace. Righteousness guards him whose way is blameless, but sin overthrows the wicked.

Proverbs 13:5-7 ESV

The one who loves the Lord is righteous, and because she has aligned her heart and mind with the will of God, hating the very things he hates, she longs for truth. In contrast, the one who lies, desiring to promote herself by tearing down others with partial truths and cleverly spun stories, is a burden to those around her. Those who live focused on the Lord and his precepts, who take care to guard their tongues and who are interested in the well-being of the entire community, will be protected by the fruit of their wise choices. In time, God will expose and judge those who perversely twist reality for their own selfish gain. Sometimes when wronged, it's best to just be silent. Although those who oppose you may rage against you and do whatever they can to form a following, ultimately God will vindicate the righteous. The sinner is no match for the Lord.

One pretends to be rich, yet has nothing; another pretends to be poor, yet has great wealth. The ransom of a man's life is his wealth, but a poor man hears no threat. The light of the righteous rejoices, but the lamp of the wicked will be put out.

Proverbs 13:7-9 ESV

Sometimes the poor, because of their passion to impress others, will do whatever they can to appear rich, living above their means and purchasing expensive items. At the same time, sometimes the wealthy pretend to lack, not sharing or giving from the resources God has blessed them with. Both are equally wrong. The rich will part with their resources if they feel their lives are in danger. The poor cannot be threatened by a bribe because they have nothing to offer. The righteous await a kingdom of never-ending bliss, but the wicked only have judgment before them. We can try to hide our financial status out of self-preservation. Either we have too little and are ashamed, or we have too much and are afraid others will take what we have. But God knows what resources he has allotted to us. Let's not lie concerning our wealth. Live simply, and be generous.

By insolence comes nothing but strife, but with those who take advice is wisdom. Wealth gained hastily will dwindle, but whoever gathers little by little will increase it. Hope deferred makes the heart sick, but a desire fulfilled is a tree of life.

Proverbs 13:10-12 ESV

The wise desire advice. Those who are prideful believe they don't need counsel, and their choices result in conflict and strife. When one acknowledges that she doesn't know everything and seeks input, her humility leads to better decisions. "Get Rich Quick" schemes and plans that involve viewing others as potential means of financial gain, are short-lived. In contrast, the one who patiently works hard, living modestly and saving for the future, will prosper. Unfulfilled hopes paralyze the heart, and the soul begins to despair. Although the righteous may not immediately have their longings fulfilled, the Lord graces his own with the ability to look forward to the future with confidence. All who put their trust in Jesus will never be put to shame. Are you feeling discouraged about your circumstances today? Do what you can to improve them, but know that for the Christian, the best is yet to come.

Whoever despises the word brings destruction on himself, but he who reveres the commandment will be rewarded. The teaching of the wise is a fountain of life, that one may turn away from the snares of death.

Proverbs 13:13-14 ESV

Those who seek out, listen to, and obey the word of the Lord will receive the reward of eternal life promised by God himself. But those who walk along the way that seems right to them, neglecting to put God's commandments into practice, will suffer greatly in the judgment. The traps of life await the fool, and she ends up the prey of many wicked schemes. In contrast, the one who responds to the teaching that comes from God enjoys fellowship with him both in this life and the life to come. Many deceptions may overcome the gullible woman. Evil people, evil desires, and evil forces are scattered along the way of those who reject the Lord, and as traps are set for hunted animals, the fool is sure to be caught by one or more of these snares. What sin easily entangles you? What are you doing to avoid its lure today?

Good sense wins favor, but the way of the treacherous is their ruin. In everything the prudent acts with knowledge, but a fool flaunts his folly. A wicked messenger falls into trouble, but a faithful envoy brings healing.

Proverbs 13:15-17 ESV

The one who hears and listens to wisdom gains favor with God and others. This person is spiritually attractive to those around her. In contrast, those who are disloyal will ultimately face rejection. The wise person is forward-thinking. She perceives what's ahead and responds with caution. She doesn't test the Lord by placing herself in compromising situations. The fool openly displays her lack of wisdom by her carelessness. The wicked messenger distorts the words of the one he represents, causing problems for the community. The faithful one brings peace when she communicates on behalf of those who sent her. Do you make your boss, your husband, or even the Lord look good to others? Or do you grumble about those in authority over you? How would you feel if everything you said yesterday were recorded and played back before those you represent? Would you be deemed a source of healing, or a channel of destruction?

Poverty and disgrace come to him who ignores instruction, but whoever heeds reproof is honored. A desire fulfilled is sweet to the soul, but to turn away from evil is an abomination to fools.

Proverbs 13:18-19 ESV

The teachable person is blessed, but the one who won't respond to correction ends up shamed. Because the fool thinks her ways are better than God's ways, she doesn't turn from destructive behavior. We can deceive ourselves into thinking that because we agree we should start or stop a behavior should be stopped or started, we are teachable. But we must include a proper response. The teachable woman listens to advice and makes changes in her views and activities. Is there any area of your life where you know you should be doing things differently, but you haven't put that knowledge into action? If so, spend the day asking God to help you to overcome your fear of either losing what isn't really best or embracing what you must do. Determine to choose the path that leads to honor by living according to God's design. In the end, you are the only one keeping yourself from doing the right thing.

Whoever walks with the wise becomes wise, but the companion of fools will suffer harm. Disaster pursues sinners, but the righteous are rewarded with good. A good man leaves an inheritance to his children's children, but the sinner's wealth is laid up for the righteous.

Proverbs 13:20-22 ESV

The one who associates with the wise, listening to instruction and following the example of godly advisors, will be wise too. The one who follows after fools will end up harming herself. The evil done by sinners will come back to haunt them, while the one who does good will be honored for her acts of kindness. The children and the grandchildren of the godly are blessed by the influence of their righteous parents, but even the riches of sinners will be squandered by their offspring. What kind of legacy will you leave for those who come after you? Will you be remembered as one who loved God and served people, or as one who chased after the pleasures of this life? In the end, those who follow the Lord, extending love and mercy to others, will be happy and honored in this life and the life to come.

The fallow ground of the poor would yield much food, but it is swept away through injustice. Whoever spares the rod hates his son, but he who loves him is diligent to discipline him. The righteous has enough to satisfy his appetite, but the belly of the wicked suffers want.

Proverbs 13:23-25 ESV

God designed the earth to produce food for its inhabitants, but because of human greed, many who desire to work hard end up unfed. Parents who truly love their children will discipline them. Why? Because the parent who wants what's best for her children knows that direction and correction are necessary to keep her kids on the right path. Unloving parents give in to the demands of their children, and in the end both the parents and the kids suffer. Those who are good and generous will be taken care of by the Lord. If the wicked appear well fed, their satisfaction will be short-lived; they will be desperate for food and water in the judgment. How well are you doing when it comes to punishing your children's wrong behavior? Do they manipulate and wear you down with tears and excuses, or are you resolved to steadfastly adhere to God's expectations for every parent?

The wisest of women builds her house, but folly with her own hands tears it down. Whoever walks in uprightness fears the Lord, but he who is devious in his ways despises him.

Proverbs 14:1-2 ESV

A godly wife does all she can to provide for the well-being of her husband and family. But without self-discipline, the unwise wife destroys whatever good God has graced her family with. The way one thinks about God is evidenced by her behavior. The one who fears the Lord lives consistently with her view of him, while the perverse woman acts according to her own desires and impulses without turning to the Lord for wisdom and instruction. So, are you a wise or a foolish woman? Do you get angry when things don't go your way and make rash decisions based on your personal feelings, or do you consider those around you and seek the good of others, even to your own hurt? It is important to take care of our families both physically and spiritually. Pray for your family, encourage them, and show them God's love today.

By the mouth of a fool comes a rod for his back, but the lips of the wise will preserve them. Where there are no oxen, the manger is clean, but abundant crops come by the strength of the ox.

Proverbs 14:3-4 ESV

In her pride, the foolish woman thinks that what she has to say is more important than the harm her words may create, and in the end, her speech brings trouble back upon her. The wise woman thoughtfully ponders whether or not she should speak what's on her mind, and considers how others might be hurt or discouraged as a result of her communication. By doing this, she avoids unnecessary pain in her life and the lives of those around her. Without livestock, an animal feeding trough may remain clean, but it's better to invest in taking care of oxen if a farmer wants to prosper. Great benefits result from the time and energy expended into gaining a harvest. Do you shrink from hard work because of effort required to produce profitable results? Learn to appreciate the "mess" that comes with being productive by doing whatever you can to make the most of every opportunity you've been given.

A faithful witness does not lie, but a false witness breathes out lies. A scoffer seeks wisdom in vain, but knowledge is easy for a man of understanding. Leave the presence of a fool, for there you do not meet words of knowledge.

Proverbs 14:5-7 ESV

The honest witness tells the truth, while the guilty speaks one lie upon the next. Although the mocker may begin to search for wisdom, her pride keeps her from humbly acknowledging herself as a creature before a holy God. Acknowledgement of God's authority allows the wise to accept his commands. We must avoid those who are foolish, although they often claim to be wise. The fool rejects the Lord and his right to rule over mankind, and many insist that an infinite and personal God doesn't exist. When they believe in a universe without a Creator, they usually forget that "no God" means no genuine meaning or purpose for human life. Yet most will agree that our souls believe in some form of absolute right or wrong, testifying to our role as image-bearers of God. Don't be deceived today. God exists, and he cares very much about what we do with our lives. Seek his will.

The wisdom of the prudent is to discern his way, but the folly of fools is deceiving. Fools mock at the guilt offering, but the upright enjoy acceptance. The heart knows its own bitterness, and no stranger shares its joy.

Proverbs 14:8-10 ESV

The wise woman gives thought to how her present actions will impact her future life. The foolish woman devises ways to harm others, not realizing that her ungodly behavior will return to her. Foolish people don't take responsibility for their sin. In fact, they resist feelings of guilt and have no desire to confess and repent of their wrongdoing. The righteous quickly ask the Lord for forgiveness when they fail to live according to his design. Only God truly knows the human heart. We have experienced joys and pains that others simply can't understand. It is unwise then to assume the motives of those around us. When we do this, we often wrongfully accuse the innocent and approve of those who are self-seeking. We must live consistently with what God has called us to, even when misunderstood by others. Be true to what the Lord has shown you and called you to today.

The house of the wicked will be destroyed, but the tent of the upright will flourish. There is a way that seems right to a man, but its end is the way to death.

Proverbs 14:11-12 ESV

A house is more stable and secure than a tent. But even the temporary and portable tent of the upright will provide more safety than the apparently permanent home of the ungodly. The proverbs frequently use the Hebrew word *derek*, which means "way." This term describes a person's overall lifestyle. One is either on the path of the righteous or the path of the wicked. Sometimes it's clear that a way will lead to destruction. But at other times, a path can deceive. It can appear to lead to safety, but in the end, leave one far from God. How can we tell which path is right? We must compare what we think and feel to what the Bible says. By examining the Scripture, laying aside our personal desires, and following the Lord's commands, we can know we will not be ashamed in the end. Genuine faith in Jesus keeps us on the proper road.

Even in laughter the heart may ache, and the end of joy may be grief. The backslider in heart will be filled with the fruit of his ways, and a good man will be filled with the fruit of his ways. The simple believes everything, but the prudent gives thought to his steps.

Proverbs 14:13-15 ESV

Though sobering, the proverbs teach that in the end our joys will meet sorrow and sadness because all must die. As long as we remain in this life, we will experience heartache. But for the righteous, a life peppered with pain will break forth into unending gladness as we dwell with God permanently in our new home. The wicked don't have this hope. The one who chooses to follow the Lord and later regrets her decision (the "backslider") will suffer as a result. In contrast, the righteous will be rewarded for her faithfulness. We must give careful thought to the choices we make. Everything we think and do creates consequences. It's important to seek the advice of others and consider our own hearts, but in the end, we know the Lord has revealed his mind to us through the written word of God. May we continually examine our behavior in light of the Scripture.

One who is wise is cautious and turns away from evil, but a fool is reckless and careless. A man of quick temper acts foolishly, and a man of evil devices is hated. The simple inherit folly, but the prudent are crowned with knowledge.

Proverbs 14:16-18 ESV

The fool doesn't think about the consequences of her actions. She makes decisions based on how she feels and what brings her pleasure. But the wise woman fears the Lord and humbly considers what God desires. The evil woman can be angry and impulsive, or calculated and manipulative. The former explodes when things don't go her way, determined to ruin those whom she considers obstacles. The latter keeps her cool, appearing levelheaded, but inwardly she's scheming to harm others. Those who accept what they hear without careful thought become fools, but the wise are determined to get more wisdom and are therefore rewarded. When things don't go your way, do you respond like the hot-head, devising ways to harm those with whom you are at odds? If you rejoice at the thought of evil befalling your enemy, ask God instead to grace you with his love for her, praying that God would draw her to himself today.

The evil bow down before the good, the wicked at the gates of the righteous. The poor is disliked even by his neighbor, but the rich has many friends.

Proverbs 14:19-20 ESV

One day, the wicked will bow before the righteous. Although God's people are often despised on earth, the time is coming when he will make things right. His enemies will be overthrown and his servants eternally blessed. Those who belong to the Lord through faith in his Son will reign and rule together with him. Sadly, many of the godly are rejected on earth because they lack beauty or material wealth. Because they aren't seen as having much to offer, the community can cast them off. Our world tends to embrace the rich, regardless of whether they seek the Lord. We may want to be around them because of what they have rather than because of who they really are. Be honest with yourself right now. Is there anyone you have secretly shunned because she lacks the things the world desires? Choose to love and support all those who love God today.

Whoever despises his neighbor is a sinner, but blessed is he who is generous to the poor. Do they not go astray who devise evil? Those who devise good meet steadfast love and faithfulness.

Proverbs 14:21-23 ESV

Every single human bears the image of God and is important to him. Those who reject and despise the unfortunate around them, withholding mercy, kindness, and even generosity when it is in their power to help, displease the Lord. But God is with the woman who is gracious toward the oppressed. Those who walk on the path of wisdom, doing good to others and obeying the Lord, will be blessed. Those who seek to harm the hurting around them cannot continue along the path of the wise. Do you look down upon or try to distance yourself from the people around you who are poor, unattractive, or just less desirable? Remember, God cares about all of humanity. Make sure you treat every person you encounter with dignity and respect, speaking truth to them in love. May each soul you cross paths with today feel as though in spending time with you, she spent time with Jesus.

June
8

*In all toil there is profit, but mere talk
tends only to poverty. The crown of the
wise is their wealth, but the folly of fools
brings folly. A truthful witness saves lives,
but one who breathes out lies is deceitful.*

Proverbs 14:24-25 ESV

Those who are willing to work hard will
prosper. But those content to ramble on about
what they are "going to do" end up with nothing.
One of the rewards of diligence is wealth. The
fool ignores wisdom and truth and ends up living
with the consequences of her unwise decisions.
The righteous person is also truthful. She
refuses to bear false testimony against another
and ends up saving the accused from wrongful
rejection or punishment. Those who spin the
truth, communicating deceptive information, end
up ruining the reputation of the innocent, even
bringing death to the one they speak against.
What about you? When you recount an incident
about someone you don't like, do you include
or omit details to make her look worse than she
actually is? If so, stop and repent today. We will
all be accountable for the harm and hurt we have
brought upon others by our deceitful words.

In the fear of the Lord one has strong confidence, and his children will have a refuge. The fear of the Lord is a fountain of life, that one may turn away from the snares of death. In a multitude of people is the glory of a king, but without people a prince is ruined.

Proverbs 14:26-28 ESV

The one who holds a high view of God, living consistently with the commands of Scripture, will be strong and secure. The offspring of this God-fearer will also benefit from the faith of her parent(s). It is critical that one have a healthy awe of God, recognizing the Lord as the Creator and Judge of heaven and earth. This fear of the Lord, which generates a humble trust in God, leads to eternal life. Those who rule must also fear God in order to wisely manage the lives entrusted to their care. The competent leader is known by the allegiance of her people. All who exercise authority must do so in a way consistent with Scripture. Whom do you lead or have authority over? Are you kind, fair, honest, thoughtful, and selfless in your management? Or do you exercise or even abandon your power for personal interests? Be careful as you oversee others today.

Whoever is slow to anger has great understanding, but he who has a hasty temper exalts folly. A tranquil heart gives life to the flesh, but envy makes the bones rot.

Proverbs 14:29-30 ESV

The wise exercise patience, controlling their emotions. They think before they speak or act, trusting in the Lord's sovereign ability to make things right, rather than craving revenge. The fool, on the other hand, refuses to hope in God and angrily demands that she immediately be vindicated for any and all offenses she incurs. Frustration and resentment end up demolishing us from the inside out. When you are upset, what do you display before those around you? Are you known to be an angry and bitter person, or one who routinely gives grace? In the end, all sin is against God, and yet the Lord waits so that as many as possible might repent and be saved. Those who are godly behave like God. May we exercise longsuffering with respect to others who have wronged us, always hoping and praying that they may turn from disobedience and choose the way that leads to life.

Whoever oppresses a poor man insults his Maker, but he who is generous to the needy honors him. The wicked is overthrown through his evildoing, but the righteous finds refuge in his death.

Proverbs 14:31-32 ESV

Those who mock, deride, or slander the poor are actually insulting the Lord, as each human bears God's image, making every life valuable. Whether beautiful or ugly, talented or simple, wealthy or destitute, because the same God has created people, all human life has worth. Thus, when we encounter another person, even the least fortunate among us, we should be moved to display kindness, treating her with dignity and respect. Since the wicked fail to give grace to the poor, they will be left without hope at the end. Those who trust in God and seek to benefit others, even putting the interests of others above their own, will live eternally. The Proverbs continually remind us that God cares about every person. Whether born or unborn, young or old, all are important to him. Those who desire godliness want to be like the Lord. Remember, God loves all people. We must love all people too.

June

12

Wisdom rests in the heart of a man of understanding, but it makes itself known even in the midst of fools. Righteousness exalts a nation, but sin is a reproach to any people. A servant who deals wisely has the king's favor, but his wrath falls on one who acts shamefully.

Proverbs 14:33-35 ESV

It's not enough to simply hear wisdom's teaching. The fool can do that. Instead, one must allow wisdom to settle into her heart and mind by implementing Scripture's principles and memorizing the words of God. But wisdom isn't only necessary for the individual. To provide peace, governments must turn to the precepts of the Lord. A morally sound nation will endure the test of time, but sin will bring even the most prosperous and powerful country down in judgment. Those who serve, whether it be the government, an employer, their families, or the Lord, must be found trustworthy, living free from scandal. When we compromise and entangle ourselves in matters outside of God's design for our lives, it brings harm to those we represent. Our sin has a way of impacting those around us. Even private transgressions damage not only our souls, but the members of our families and our communities as well.

A soft answer turns away wrath, but a harsh word stirs up anger. The tongue of the wise commends knowledge, but the mouths of fools pour out folly. The eyes of the Lord are in every place, keeping watch on the evil and the good.

Proverbs 15:1-3 ESV

The Proverbs teach that every person has the ability to exercise self-control when it comes to what she says and the way she says it. The words we use, even the tone of our speech, greatly impact the way our communication is received. We are never to compromise truth, but to be kind when working with those who have a difference of opinion. It's not wise to couple a painful message with a harsh tone. Through gentleness, the wise make knowledge attractive and desirable. Fools, refusing to exercise self-control, spew out words that bring harm rather than healing. God is aware of all that we communicate, the attitude of our words, and even the motives behind what we say. Not one thing in the universe escapes the knowledge of God. He will reward those who build others up, and he will hold responsible those who tear down people, relationship, and even communities.

A gentle tongue is a tree of life, but perverseness in it breaks the spirit. A fool despises his father's instruction, but whoever heeds reproof is prudent.

Proverbs 15:4-5 ESV

Kind words bring healing and life to the person who has been broken by the harsh and insensitive language of careless and even selfish people. We know whether one is a fool by observing the way she listens to, implements, and stores up wisdom. Those who pay attention to correction, humbly making changes and growing more like the Lord, are wise. The fool sees no need to improve her character. She doesn't want to put in the effort to make changes. We must be extremely careful about what we say. It's easy to let harmful speech roll out of our mouths, but it's difficult to undo the damage created by foolish talk. Think of a time when you spoke about another in a mean-spirited way. Ask God to forgive you and cleanse you from your sinful speech, working diligently with the Holy Spirit to be wise with your words today.

In the house of the righteous there is much treasure, but trouble befalls the income of the wicked. The lips of the wise spread knowledge; not so the hearts of fools.

Proverbs 15:6-7 ESV

The upright wisely steward God's gifts while they enjoy the blessing of helping others. Those who are evil keep their resources to themselves. Both ill-gotten and hoarded finances provide no real long-term benefit for the people who hold them. The righteous are not only generous with their money, but gracious with their speech too. Fools don't have insightful words to share. When they speak, what comes forth is not consistent with Scripture and holds no lasting value. Do your words spiritually benefit those who hear them? One's speech betrays the nature of her heart. If you were declared wise or foolish based on the words you spoke in the last week, what would the verdict be? Be careful to think before you talk. When in doubt about what you're about to say, better to be silent than sorry.

The sacrifice of the wicked is an abomination to the Lord, but the prayer of the upright is acceptable to him. The way of the wicked is an abomination to the Lord, but he loves him who pursues righteousness.

Proverbs 15:8-10 ESV

God accepts the prayers of the righteous, but rejects even the sacrifice of the wicked. When offering a sacrifice to the Lord, the believer brought an animal in humble obedience. In contrast, the wicked would bring offerings in an attempt to manipulate God to do as they pleased. They believed if they gave God what he wanted, he would have to respond to their cries for help. And yet, they refused to give God their lives. They wanted to live according to their own desires while enjoying the favor of the Lord. But God is with those who seek him and his righteousness. The one who longs for God will be graced with all she needs in this life and rewarded in the next. When you pray or serve the Lord, do you assume he is obligated to you as a result? Or do you worship because it is the right thing to do?

There is severe discipline for him who forsakes the way; whoever hates reproof will die. Sheol and Abaddon lie open before the Lord; how much more the hearts of the children of man! A scoffer does not like to be reproved; he will not go to the wise.

Proverbs 15:10-12 ESV

In the end, the ultimate consequence for rejecting the way of the Lord is eternal death. This doesn't mean that one will cease to exist, but instead the soul will live forever in a place where she is shut out from the presence of God and his Son Jesus. God is aware of everything that occurs in the universe, including what takes place in the depths of hell. Nothing escapes his notice. Though veiled to other humans, God sees the motives behind every person's thoughts, intentions, and actions. The fool does not receive advice and correction, but is determined to do what she feels is right. We should remember that God is concerned not only with what we do, but why we do what we do as well. If we are honest, we must admit that we are often driven by selfish desires. Ask God to cleanse you from your sinful motives today, aligning your heart with his.

A glad heart makes a cheerful face, but by sorrow of heart the spirit is crushed. The heart of him who has understanding seeks knowledge, but the mouths of fools feed on folly. All the days of the afflicted are evil, but the cheerful of heart has a continual feast.

Proverbs 15:13-15 ESV

How we feel inwardly is often reflected in our countenance. When the heart is joyful, so is the face, and when the soul is broken, discouragement and depression result. The wise person works to gain information before forming a judgment. The fool is confident that her opinion alone matters, and she seeks out others who agree with her rather than those who uphold the standard of the Lord. If evil men prosper, their ability to truly enjoy this life is inhibited by the general wretchedness that results from disobedience to the Lord. Although the godly may have issues with health, relationships, and finances, their hope in God and his word allows them to navigate the difficulties of this life with joy. What about you? When your circumstances are tough, are you miserable? If so, fix your heart on what is true. Let your sorrow turn to joy as you contemplate your relationship with the Lord of this universe.

Better is a little with the fear of the Lord than great treasure and trouble with it. Better is a dinner of herbs where love is than a fattened ox and hatred with it.

Proverbs 15:16-17 ESV

"Life isn't fair" is a saying used to encourage others and ourselves when things don't work out the way they should. We know that ungodly people are often blessed, while the righteous suffer. Yet it is better to have a small amount of wealth and be a child of God than to have an abundance and exist in the turmoil that results from placing our hope in this present life. Loving and being loved surpasses even the most desirable of circumstances coupled with hatred. How could those who are materially blessed be hateful? We all have the potential to drift down the path of hate. When we become selfish, bitter about past hurt feelings, unforgiving, and envious, we can be hateful people. But when we embrace God's love and can freely extend his love toward all those he places in our lives, we are living rightly. Choose love by letting go of self today.

A hot-tempered man stirs up strife, but he who is slow to anger quiets contention. The way of a sluggard is like a hedge of thorns, but the path of the upright is a level highway. A wise son makes a glad father, but a foolish man despises his mother.

Proverbs 15:18-20 ESV

Success is often determined by one's ability to control her emotions. Many foolish people think they must continually respond to their feelings to be genuine, but reacting to impulses, urges, and desires rather than exercising self-discipline is unwise. Those who don't control anger and resentment create chaos, while the patient woman brings calm to the people around her. Laziness is also an obstacle to a prosperous life. The diligent person minimizes hindrances to achievement by hard work and determination. The son who puts God's wisdom into practice, making choices consistent with biblical principles, brings joy to godly parents, but the foolish son ignores instruction, wrongly thinking he knows best. How well do you manage your emotions? Are you driven and ruled by bitterness, passion, lust, or rage? Allow the real you to be in charge of your feelings today, making good choices consistent with God's design for human life, rather than being fueled by impulses and whims.

Folly is a joy to him who lacks sense, but a man of understanding walks straight ahead. Without counsel plans fail, but with many advisers they succeed.

Proverbs 15:21-22 ESV

The wise person stays on the path of righteousness because she desires the good result. The fool is driven by her emotions and only considers what will make her feel happy in the moment. She doesn't care about long-term consequences because she has no fear of the Lord. Those who are humble admit that they need the advice of others. The arrogant don't seek counsel. They are actually self-righteous, believing their conclusions are right. When you are making decisions, do you seek the wisdom of God? The first place to start is with the Scripture. What does the Bible say about the current choices you are facing? At the same time, be sure and seek the Lord's help in prayer. Then go to a few close friends who know God and ask for their input. Though it may be awkward and embarrassing, the advice we get from others can be vital when it comes to intelligent decision-making.

To make an apt answer is a joy to a man, and a word in season, how good it is! The path of life leads upward for the prudent, that he may turn away from Sheol beneath.

Proverbs 15:23-24 ESV

Those who provide biblical answers are a source of joy to others. We can become confused about our roles in marriage, how we parent, choices at work or school, how to be an effective friend, our investment in eternal things, how to love Jesus, and even the character of God and humanity. Thoughts compete in our minds all day, every day. Many wind up off the path of righteousness and in a ditch by relying solely on themselves to navigate through life properly. The path of life keeps us away from destruction. When questions arise, how wonderful it is to receive sound and sensible instruction through the wisdom of another. It can be exhausting to minister to others, explaining truth while calming their fears, but the payoff is well worth it. The one who takes time to instruct and encourage others is like an oasis in the dry desert of doubt and unbelief.

The Lord tears down the house of the proud but maintains the widow's boundaries. The thoughts of the wicked are an abomination to the Lord, but gracious words are pure. Whoever is greedy for unjust gain troubles his own household, but he who hates bribes will live.

Proverbs 15:25-27 ESV

Ancient boundary markers were used to designate personal property lines. Those who were crooked would slightly but continually move these land markers, and over long periods of time, the deceptive would end up with more than they legitimately owned. But God protects even the widow, left without a husband, against the arrogant crook. The Lord detests the deceitful practices of the wicked. The intentions and the words of the upright, who have no selfish agendas, are of great worth in the eyes of God. The greedy woman is self-destructive, setting herself against the Lord. The woman who rejects flattery, manipulation, and shady financial conduct is wise. In the end, she and her family will be blessed. Are you honest when it comes to financial transactions? Do you pay what you owe and give as you should? Even if no one else sees you taking what doesn't really belong to you, God does.

The heart of the righteous ponders how to answer, but the mouth of the wicked pours out evil things. The Lord is far from the wicked, but he hears the prayer of the righteous. The light of the eyes rejoices the heart, and good news refreshes the bones.

Proverbs 15:28-30 ESV

The wicked and righteous can be distinguished by their speech. The one who considers others thinks carefully about her words and the impact they will make. The self-centered person blurts out harmful words, often rooted in hurt feelings and bitterness. When the wicked are mad, everyone is going to hear about it. God draws close to the righteous, listening to her prayers of repentance and requests for help, but he doesn't extend this help to the evil. Good news brings joy to the heart and the soul, and the gospel brings abundant joy to all who believe. How do you handle yourself when your feelings are hurt? Do you allow resentment to build up until you unleash bitter words in a fury? Or do you consider that God may be orchestrating your disappointments to make you more like his Son? When you are tempted to vent your anger today, make sure it's truly for the good of all concerned.

The ear that listens to life-giving reproof will dwell among the wise. Whoever ignores instruction despises himself, but he who listens to reproof gains intelligence. The fear of the Lord is instruction in wisdom, and humility comes before honor.

Proverbs 15:31-33 ESV

The one who listens and responds to God's word is considered wise. The person who refuses to put the teaching of the Lord into practice is in essence committing suicide, hating herself by ensuring her own eternal death. To be wise, one must fear the Lord and be willing to submit to his design for human life. We must humbly acknowledge that we need God's help. We are foolish if we believe that we know or understand more than God does. When we reject his truth, it's like we are saying, "Thanks for the advice, God, but my ways are better than yours." Even though things may not make perfect sense to us, appear the way we think they should, or even feel as fun or comfortable as we would like them to, God knows exactly what is best. The wise person recognizes this truth, admits her own limitations, and makes her choices consistent with Scripture.

June

26

The plans of the heart belong to man, but the answer of the tongue is from the Lord. All the ways of a man are pure in his own eyes, but the Lord weighs the spirit.

Proverbs 16:1-2 ESV

Although people orchestrate plans in their hearts, God is in charge of what actually comes off the tongue. Though this may seem odd, the account of Balaam's attempt to curse Israel while God caused him to bless the nation (Numbers 23:11-12) illustrates God's sovereignty and the tension between man's plans and the will of the Lord. God not only evaluates a human's actions, but thoughts as well. God's standard of righteousness is far above anything we can achieve. Even our best attempts at upright behavior fall short. We are all dependent upon the mercy and grace of God to cover our transgressions. Our bad and our good works need to be washed by the blood of Jesus. Nevertheless, God is pleased when we align both our deeds and thoughts with his will. So instead of simply asking yourself what you will do today, ask why you will do it as well.

Commit your work to the Lord, and your plans will be established. The Lord has made everything for its purpose, even the wicked for the day of trouble. Everyone who is arrogant in heart is an abomination to the Lord; be assured, he will not go unpunished.

Proverbs 16:3-5 ESV

The Hebrew verb translated as "commit" in verse 3 is interesting. It means "to roll" or "to roll away." The wise woman is called to roll her work, her endeavors, and her life away from herself and to the Lord. Only then can she live peacefully, knowing that God is in control, orchestrating everything together for his purposes. Even the actions of evil people are not outside of God's sovereign reign. Those who consider themselves above God, rejecting his design for human life, will face the judgment of the Lord. If you are feeling stressed, tired, or weary today, then mentally picture yourself taking your life and rolling it like a huge boulder before the throne of God. After that, leave the boulder there. The plans and actions of those who are dependent upon the Lord are entrusted to a good God who cares deeply for all who belong to him.

June
28

By steadfast love and faithfulness iniquity is atoned for, and by the fear of the Lord one turns away from evil. When a man's ways please the Lord, he makes even his enemies to be at peace with him.

Proverbs 16:6-7 ESV

When a woman recognizes her sin, putting her trust in the Lord, he rewires her from the inside out and causes her to love him and love others. Her new nature demonstrates that she has been released from the penalty of her sin. Once pardoned, her desire to please the Lord compels her to continue in the way of love, worshipping God and serving people. There is nothing greater than the knowing that we are pleasing the Lord. No matter how deeply entrenched in darkness, God can lift the repentant sinner from the grave and place her, blameless, before his throne. If you have experienced God's forgiveness, you are free to live for his glory. Your battle is no longer an earthly one. With whom are you at war today? If you have been reconciled to God, seek to be reconciled to your enemies. If they continue to reject you, trust God to make things right.

Better is a little with righteousness than great revenues with injustice. The heart of man plans his way, but the Lord establishes his steps. An oracle is on the lips of a king; his mouth does not sin in judgment.

Proverbs 16:8-10 ESV

Often, those who live ungodly lives enjoy financial prosperity. But it is better to be righteous and have little than to enjoy a godless life, even if it includes riches. People can scheme all they want, but in the end God is the one who decides where they will go. The wise king declares just verdicts when making decisions and trying cases. The Lord uses the godly king as his mouthpiece. And yet, every king has moral shortcomings and failures. But only one King did the will of the Lord. In every thought, attitude, and action, he obeyed the God who sent him into the world. This righteous King Jesus will rule over his kingdom in a place he is preparing for himself and his servants. Take a few minutes to talk to your good King today. Let him know how grateful you are that because he is faithful you are secure eternally.

A just balance and scales are the Lord's; all the weights in the bag are his work. It is an abomination to kings to do evil, for the throne is established by righteousness. Righteous lips are the delight of a king, and he loves him who speaks what is right.

Proverbs 16:11-13 ESV

Balances and beams were used in the marketplace to weigh goods and monies, enabling fair transactions. Because God created our universe as an ordered system, he expects us to live consistently with physical and spiritual laws. When a ruler uses his authority for selfish gain, he opposes the Lord and will eventually fall. But the honest king strengthens his throne when he leans upon God's wisdom. The Lord honors the upright king, and the king responds to upright subjects. The one who speaks the truth and doesn't manipulate the facts is a joy to the king. All men value a truth-teller, yet honesty often comes with a price tag. The honest person may have to bring bad news, confess she did wrong, or risk being seen as ordinary. And yet it is good to be honest. Pray that God would help you to speak truthfullly today. Don't let fear keep you from doing the right thing.

A king's wrath is a messenger of death, and a wise man will appease it. In the light of a king's face there is life, and his favor is like the clouds that bring the spring rain.

Proverbs 16:14-15 ESV

When wrong has transpired and the king is angry, punishment, even death, may result. But the king's fury can be satisfied by the humble and gentle words of the godly. The wise person will confess, repent, and appeal to the king for mercy. When the king is pleased, he grants grace, bringing life to the one he favors. And so it is with the Lord. The people of ancient Israel often prayed to the Lord, asking him to cause his face to shine upon them, granting them salvation. Has the Lord allowed you to humbly confess your sin, casting yourself upon him alone for mercy? If so, then he has caused his face to shine upon you and graced you with eternal life. No matter how hectic your day may be, rejoice in the favor you have received. The King of Heaven has selected you personally to be the recipient of his goodness. Things don't get better than that!

How much better to get wisdom than gold! To get understanding is to be chosen rather than silver. The highway of the upright turns aside from evil; whoever guards his way preserves his life.

Proverbs 16:16-17 ESV

The Proverbs remind the reader again about the benefit and necessity of gaining wisdom. The upright will pursue the instruction of the Lord, as nothing is more valuable than wisdom. Though wealth may provide comfort and ease in this life, wisdom allows one to thrive eternally. When ancient travelers journeyed along marked roads and noticed an attractive city along the way, they would deviate from the highway, taking a side route to get to the new location. The one who is upright continues on the highway of wisdom, rejecting any lure a side road may offer. What temptation is pulling at you and enticing you today? Is anything causing you to stray from your course? If so, don't look to the right or the left, but instead, keep on walking straight ahead. Whatever offer requires you to depart from God's good path is simply not worth it.

Pride goes before destruction, and a haughty spirit before a fall. It is better to be of a lowly spirit with the poor than to divide the spoil with the proud.

Proverbs 16:18-19 ESV

The arrogant think they know more than others, even more than God, and are determined to do things according to their own understanding. Because they resist God's good counsel, they will ultimately end up broken and empty. Pride is so destructive that it's better to have nothing in this life than to share in the wealth and riches of those who are arrogant. God sees the ways of both the proud and the humble. He will not let those who are oppressed by the haughty suffer long. When we meet death, everything changes. Those who despise the Lord will be shut out from his presence, while those who patiently wait for his deliverance will be richly rewarded. When tempted to take things into your own hands today, wait upon the Lord. He gives grace to the humble. Listen to his word, apply biblical truth to the situations you face, and trust him to make things right.

Whoever gives thought to the word will discover good, and blessed is he who trusts in the Lord. The wise of heart is called discerning, and sweetness of speech increases persuasiveness. Good sense is a fountain of life to him who has it, but the instruction of fools is folly.

Proverbs 16:20-22 ESV

The wise woman gives attention to the Scripture and is blessed as a result. She is careful concerning what she speaks and watches her words, making sure they are consistent with the teaching that comes from God. The wise woman also uses her words to persuade others to consider their own behavior. She encourages them to make good decisions that will lead to a life without regrets. Those who are righteous provide words of life as they instruct others to align their choices with biblical law and principle. When we bring God's truth to the people he has placed in our sphere of influence, we can be a catalyst for spiritual growth in their lives. Help others to consider the choices they must make. What will be the outcome of their behavior one hundred years from now? Be consistent with advice you give, living out everything you say and do in light of eternity.

The heart of the wise makes his speech judicious and adds persuasiveness to his lips. Gracious words are like a honeycomb, sweetness to the soul and health to the body.

Proverbs 16:23-24 ESV

The wise woman gives much thought to what she does and doesn't say. If her heart is humble before God, open to correction and instruction, she is able to respond with thoughtful speech regardless of the position she's placed in. Words driven by love for others are like honey, both sweet and healing. They bring life to individuals and communities. Those around us can be damaged by the harsh and thoughtless speech of the foolish. The wise woman navigates around those statements and helps the hearer regain hope. The Proverbs remind us how we must restrain our speech. At the same time, we must carefully consider how to communicate with kind and healing words. There are times when we should hold back our thoughts and times when we should speak them, even when it's hard. Have you used your words for good lately? Ask God to grace you with words that build others up today.

July
6

There is a way that seems right to a man, but its end is the way to death. A worker's appetite works for him; his mouth urges him on. A worthless man plots evil, and his speech is like a scorching fire.

Proverbs 16:25-27 ESV

The proud person refuses to see her need for God's wisdom, instruction, and ultimately his forgiveness. She erroneously believes she knows what's best, owes no account to God for her sinful behavior, and possibly even deserves reward in the judgment because she is a "good person." God will decide she is a "good person." Our need for food drives us to work hard. Although we may work for others, in the end we satisfy our own wants. A longing for spiritual truth drives those who are righteous to seek the Lord. The worthless person uses her words to disparage others and invent ways to circulate that information in the community. She is like one who prepares scorching food or throws flaming spears, burning members of the community. She takes pleasure in seeing ruin befall another. The wise person will avoid this woman. The destructive fire she creates is in the end driven by the flames of hell.

A dishonest man spreads strife, and a whisperer separates close friends. A man of violence entices his neighbor and leads him in a way that is not good. Whoever winks his eyes plans dishonest things; he who purses his lips brings evil to pass.

Proverbs 16:28-30 ESV

The ungodly woman is determined to speak her mind. She spreads dirt on her neighbor in an attempt to destroy relationships. The whisperer pretends she's only quietly telling a select few about her victim. She lowers her voice and maligns in secret, hoping to destroy reputations. The whisperer and the listener are both at fault. The violent woman is determined to get others to on her side. She isn't satisfied until she's brought down as many as she can. If she's unhappy, everyone else will be too. Using her eyes and mouth, she signals behind her victim's back. Her target is unaware of the scheme that's been mounted against her. Many have been brought down and ruined by such women. But groans to God for help do not go unheard. Everything that's been spoken in secret will be shouted from the rooftops, and the one who has humbly put her hope in the Lord will be vindicated.

Gray hair is a crown of glory; it is gained in a righteous life. Whoever is slow to anger is better than the mighty, and he who rules his spirit than he who takes a city. The lot is cast into the lap, but its every decision is from the Lord.

Proverbs 16:31-33 ESV

Old age should be treated with respect. The older woman has experienced more days of life and is generally able to see the wisdom of embracing God's design for human behavior. The one who is wise is able to control her anger. This godly woman thinks about others before she reacts. She refrains from impulsive outbursts. She rules her spirit by taking control of her own emotions, overlooking the foolish statements and actions of others. She is not paralyzed by hurt feelings. Her trust is in the Lord, and she knows that every decision is ultimately from the hand of her good God. Until you agree that you wrestle not against flesh and blood, you will be chained by others' opinions of you. What's keeping you from being or becoming the heroine in full control of her emotions? Let go of all bitterness today. Extend kindness to everyone, even those who aren't so kind to you.

Better is a dry morsel with quiet than a house full of feasting with strife. A servant who deals wisely will rule over a son who acts shamefully and will share the inheritance as one of the brothers.

Proverbs 17:1-2 ESV

A dry piece of bread alone, without oil, vinegar, or even butter, served in the presence of security and love, is better than a wonderful banquet accompanied by fighting. A humble lifestyle with harmony surpasses all the world's goods. A birthright is not the only criteria for determining an inheritance. The faithful servant will often receive as much if not more than the natural-born son. Healthy relationships are of more value than material stuff. If you don't have much when it comes to finances, but you have strong family bonds, good friends, and are connected with brothers and sisters in Christ, then you are blessed. Appreciate the things that money can't buy and a lack of money can't lose. If you have no godly relationships, get involved in a ministry at your church. Make your life about serving others. You will have treasure in this life and the next one.

The crucible is for silver, and the furnace is for gold, and the Lord tests hearts. An evildoer listens to wicked lips, and a liar gives ear to a mischievous tongue.

Proverbs 17:3-4 ESV

When intense heat is applied to metals, they become liquid and can be separated into their components. Silver and gold are purified from contamination through fire. In the same way, God tests the human heart. When experiencing the heat of trials, we can discover whether or not our faith is genuine. And as shocking as it may seem, the woman who listens to gossip and slander is just as guilty as the one who maligns others. A woman may think she is justified by providing a listening ear, but this proverb calls her a liar. When we stand before the judgment seat of Christ, we will be tested. And if we have spoken or listened to destructive speech, participating in the harm of another human's reputation, we will be found guilty. When there is none to hear, evil speech dies out. Be extremely careful of what you say and what you listen to today. God is concerned with both!

Whoever mocks the poor insults his Maker; he who is glad at calamity will not go unpunished. Grandchildren are the crown of the aged, and the glory of children is their fathers.

Proverbs 17:5-6 ESV

All humans bear the image of their Creator, and every person has great worth in the sight of God. Those who look down at the poor, treating them with disdain, are actually standing against the God who made them. Anyone who takes secret pleasure in the downfall of another will be punished. Obedient children and grandchildren are like a crown worn by the elderly. And children prize godly parents. God values the family unit. How often do we feel justified when we hear that misfortune has struck our enemies? We can easily overlook our arrogance, forgetting that only God has made us differ from any other soul, including those with whom we are at odds with. Examine your attitude toward your enemies today. If God reveals any darkness in you, ask him to cleanse you from all selfishness. Extend compassion to all people, not only the ones you enjoy.

Fine speech is not becoming to a fool; still less is false speech to a prince. A bribe is like a magic stone in the eyes of the one who gives it; wherever he turns he prospers. Whoever covers an offense seeks love, but he who repeats a matter separates close friends.

Proverbs 17:7-9 ESV

Those in positions of authority are counted on by their communities to be trustworthy. Leaders must refrain from any temptation to lie. Just as eloquent speech doesn't typify the fool, those who rule should not be characterized by speaking untruthfully. A bribe has the power to influence decisions and choices, and those who use bribery will often successfully manipulate the wicked. But God will not show favoritism to any, and so the woman who seeks the Lord refuses to show partiality as well. The righteous woman promotes forgiveness and reconciliation between the members of her community. The wicked woman uses gossip to destroy relationships. She continually repeats the wrongdoing of others and is pleased when friendships end. God desires his people to live together in harmony. Think about your conversations over the last week. Are you one who promotes love or strife? What would your family, friends, and neighbors say? Why not ask?

A rebuke goes deeper into a man of understanding than a hundred blows into a fool. An evil man seeks only rebellion, and a cruel messenger will be sent against him. Let a man meet a she-bear robbed of her cubs rather than a fool in his folly.

Proverbs 17:10-12 ESV

Instead of gossiping, the godly woman will confront a wrongdoer. The wise one in error will listen and receive correction. But the foolish do not respond to good counsel, in fact, even extreme measures fail to generate repentance within the fool. The evil woman is determined to do things her own way, bowing her heart before none. But God's angel will one day settle the score. The Syrian Brown Bear could be found in the forests of ancient Israel. When the female bear had her cubs with her, she was fierce, doing whatever she could to protect her offspring. It would be idiotic to challenge the mother bear that had just been robbed of her cubs. In the same way, the fool becomes enraged when she doesn't get her way. This impulsive person is unstable and will gladly bring down an entire community to prove her point. Don't become foolish by failing to control your anger today.

July
14

If anyone returns evil for good, evil will not depart from his house. The beginning of strife is like letting out water, so quit before the quarrel breaks out. He who justifies the wicked and he who condemns the righteous are both alike an abomination to the Lord.

Proverbs 17:13-15 ESV

The Lord will punish those who respond with harm when offered kindness. A dam holds back water, but a small crack in the structure can cause a flood. In the same way, when the fool engages in a fight, a few words can escalate into a full brawl. Better to keep one's mouth shut than allow anger to become sinful speech. God hates injustice. Those who allow the guilty to go free and the innocent to be punished are displeasing to him. We may not blatantly return evil for good, but do so subtly. Have you been unappreciative of a gift or dismissed an invitation from one who sought to do good to you? Have you ignored attempts of family members to spend time with you? When others are kind, don't snub them in return. God is aware of everything that happens in heaven and on earth. Let's not be foolish by trampling over those around us.

Why should a fool have money in his hand to buy wisdom when he has no sense? A friend loves at all times, and a brother is born for adversity.

Proverbs 17:16-17 ESV

It would be dumb to believe that one can buy true love by hiring a prostitute. In the same way, the fool wrongly believes she can purchase wisdom. But wisdom won't be sold. She is available without cost, yet will only reveal herself to those who seek, listen to, and apply her insights. The benefits wisdom offers to the faithful come without charge. Not only is it wrong to gossip, but it is also wrong to reject a friend. A genuine friend sticks by her neighbor, even when it includes suffering. The one who abandons her friend was never a friend to begin with. The friend of Jesus has been forgiven an unpardonable debt and brought into communion with the King of the universe, although she did nothing to earn her status. This godly woman will extend grace to those around her, sticking by her friends through thick and thin, mirroring what the Lord has done for her.

One who lacks sense gives a pledge and puts up security in the presence of his neighbor. Whoever loves transgression loves strife; he who makes his door high seeks destruction. A man of crooked heart does not discover good, and one with a dishonest tongue falls into calamity.

Proverbs 17:18-20 ESV

Although it's important to be a good friend, it's foolish to guarantee a creditor that another will pay back loaned money. To put yourself in a position of struggling to pay off your friend's debt should she default is unwise. The person who seeks to elevate herself above her neighbors, building a high door, is also unwise, as God opposes those who are prideful. The woman with a twisted heart is betrayed by her ungodly speech. To promote herself, she lies about others, tearing down people with her words. By trashing the reputation of others, she believes she will be lifted up. But in the end, the one who disparages her neighbors betrays the darkness of her heart. Your words are the thermometer of your heart. Based on what you've said in the last week, is your heart warm or cold? If you don't like the answer, ask God to change you from the inside out.

He who sires a fool gets himself sorrow, and the father of a fool has no joy. A joyful heart is good medicine, but a crushed spirit dries up the bones.

Proverbs 17:21-22 ESV

The foolish child brings grief to herself and to her parents. Her father laments her unwise choices. But wisdom advises one to live joyfully, looking for and focusing on the good in every situation. By doing so, the heart is graced with vitality rather than broken under despair. One who is depressed loses her passion for living. Jesus taught his disciples that because their names were recorded in the Book of Life, they had great reason for joy. It's inconsistent with God's call upon believers' lives to remain discouraged. When we focus on our problems, we can feel overwhelmed, but when we get our eyes and our hearts looking upward, we remember we have everything to gain, and nothing to lose. If you are feeling sorrowful, ask God to help you consider your great salvation. And then, move your attention off yourself and onto others, lifting the spirits of those around you today.

The wicked accepts a bribe in secret to pervert the ways of justice. The discerning sets his face toward wisdom, but the eyes of a fool are on the ends of the earth.

Proverbs 17:23-24 ESV

Those who are evil use bribery to get what they want. They aren't concerned with fairness, but instead make sure decisions rule in their favor. To maintain reputations, they keep their bribes hidden, so that none but the parties involved knows what transpired. The foolish woman desires things that are unrealistic, like "the ends of the earth." Her focus is not on her home, workplace, community, and church. Instead, she sees herself as superior to the average person, navigating through life by her own set of rules. The wise woman is a team player. She thinks about how she can glorify God in the arenas of life he has called her to. What are your short and long term goals? Are they attainable? There's nothing wrong with determination, but if we make our ambitions too lofty, we end up accomplishing nothing. The long run is a series of small steps. Challenge yourself within reason today.

A foolish son is a grief to his father and bitterness to her who bore him. To impose a fine on a righteous man is not good, nor to strike the noble for their uprightness.

Proverbs 17:25-26 ESV

The son who doesn't listen to wisdom, following after his sinful desires, taking shortcuts whenever possible, wronging others, lying, manipulating, and constantly prowling for more, brings great distress to his godly parents. The mother and father who actually encourage his self-seeking and godless ways are just as foolish as the son they bore. Those in authority who allow the innocent to be punished are in the wrong. Whether they receive unfair fines or a physical beating, God sees when the righteous are abused. Are you suffering because of the mistreatment of a family member, friend, co-worker, or even an enemy? Although it can be incredibly painful, choose to see God's hand in the situation. God will work the circumstances for your good and see that the wrongdoer is held accountable for his wickedness. God is good and will make everything right in the end.

Whoever restrains his words has knowledge, and he who has a cool spirit is a man of understanding. Even a fool who keeps silent is considered wise: when he closes his lips, he is deemed intelligent.

Proverbs 17:27-28 ESV

A woman's wisdom is revealed by the way she manages her speech. She keeps herself back from responding unwisely, even when provoked. She is patient, calm, and employs words with extreme self-control. Because the wise have learned the art of controlling their emotions, even the foolish woman can appear discerning when she keeps her mouth shut. When we hear a woman "going off" on a rant or exploding hotly in a difficult situation, we don't assume her to be righteous. When we read internet posts from others about how they were wronged or cheated, or when subtle yet public statements jab at another's character on social media, our heart breaks, and rightfully so. Be careful of what you say and what you post or even comment on. The godly woman thinks through the impact of every word, spoken or printed, reflecting her desire to please Jesus and others rather than herself.

Whoever isolates himself seeks his own desire; he breaks out against all sound judgment. A fool takes no pleasure in understanding, but only in expressing his opinion.

Proverbs 18:1-2 ESV

The fool separates himself from others. He loves to indulge in selfish desires and doesn't want anyone telling him what to do. It is unwise and ungodly to remove yourself from the influence of your family, friends, and church. Isolation leads to unreasonable attitudes. The fool has no desire to discern between wrong and right behavior. He goes with what he feels like doing. Although he continually expresses his thoughts and opinions, he isn't interested in advice. He thinks he is right and everyone else is wrong. The fool believes he is truly different and can play by his own rules. But the day will come when he stands before the throne of God only to discover that he isn't all that unique. His disobedience will sentence him to the place of ultimate isolation with weeping and gnashing of teeth. Don't hide today. Instead, get up, get out, and make things right with God and with others.

When wickedness comes, contempt comes also, and with dishonor comes disgrace. The words of a man's mouth are deep waters; the fountain of wisdom is a bubbling brook. It is not good to be partial to the wicked or to deprive the righteous of justice.

Proverbs 18:3-5 ESV

Because the fool rejects wisdom, he will experience the judgment of God and his community. His failure to exercise self-control and passion for self-indulgence cause him to be viewed with disrespect. The words and ideas of a careless person can be as dangerous as deep water, but the speech that comes from the righteous is like a rushing stream, refreshing the souls of others by allowing them be recharged and renewed. Those who excuse wicked behavior, possibly due to a bribe, are not pleasing to the Lord. Nor are those who don't treat the godly with fairness. Though we may not take bribes, we may approve of the ungodly and their sinful ways so that we can be accepted by them. But God knows what we are doing and why we are doing it. Don't compromise what you know to be true in order to gain approval from the world. It never pays off in the end.

A fool's lips walk into a fight, and his mouth invites a beating. A fool's mouth is his ruin, and his lips are a snare to his soul. The words of a whisperer are like delicious morsels; they go down into the inner parts of the body.

Proverbs 18:6-8 ESV

The fool's thoughtless speech incites conflict. He carelessly blurts out whatever he feels like saying, justifying himself when others respond with hurt or anger. "Why should I not be able to say whatever I want?" he reasons, and soon a fight breaks out. His words become a trap, but in the end he is the one ensnared as he suffers the consequences of his impulsive and inconsiderate speech. And worse than the words of a fool are those of a gossip. The gossip ruins the reputation of others, even damaging relationships between friends. The tidbits of information the gossip "quietly" provides are hard to resist, enticing others to listen. But once heard, they permanently damage the hearer and the victim. It's not easy to walk away from the lure of gossip, but it's the right thing to do. Once you have heard a slanderous report about another, put an end to the damage by not repeating the news.

Whoever is slack in his work is a brother to him who destroys. The name of the Lord is a strong tower; the righteous man runs into it and is safe. A rich man's wealth is his strong city, and like a high wall in his imagination.

Proverbs 18:9-11 ESV

The one who is slack procrastinates, putting off what she knows she needs to do. Because she doesn't tackle her work head-on, it's as if she allowed a thief or a destroyer to plunder her stuff. But in reality, she is the criminal, stealing from herself. The character of our God is our protection and provision. When attacked by the gossip or the slanderer, the righteous woman purposefully turns to the Lord, fully trusting him to make things right. She clings to the promises of his word and is at peace. In contrast, the ungodly person puts her trust in her possessions and even her earthly relationships. But when the hour of judgment comes, she will find they fail to protect her from harm in this life and the next. The foolish woman anchors her faith in what she sees, while the godly woman rivets her hope in the invisible but all-present God.

Before destruction a man's heart is haughty, but humility comes before honor. If one gives an answer before he hears, it is his folly and shame.

Proverbs 18:12-13 ESV

The arrogant and the humble are placed in contrast to one another. The Lord will honor the humble woman, as she genuinely seeks the welfare of others. But the prideful person lifts her agenda above the needs of those around her. It doesn't matter who is offended, as long as she gets her way. Having never understood her need for mercy or taken hold of the grace of God, she doesn't understand how to extend kindness to others. Even in conversation, she refuses to listen, yet is always eager to throw out what she thinks and her opinion about how things should be done. Immersed in her self-centered thoughts, she fails to learn from those around her, actually seeing herself as superior. The next time you communicate with someone, pay attention long enough to hear God's wisdom through her life experience. May we be less anxious to speak and more determined to listen today.

A man's spirit will endure sickness, but a crushed spirit who can bear? An intelligent heart acquires knowledge, and the ear of the wise seeks knowledge. A man's gift makes room for him and brings him before the great.

Proverbs 18:14-16 ESV

Wise thinking allows the human spirit to endure sickness, but there isn't much hope for the spiritually depressed. When the inner man is beaten down by discouragement, the soul tends to just give up. We must pursue knowledge. We can't wait for wisdom to come to us, but must seek after her, putting her instruction into practice. Though a gift may provide access to someone greater in social standing, the righteous should avoid bribes as they ultimately pervert justice. Many great men and women have faced spiritual depression. It is a tool of the enemy to overwhelm the soul, keeping the Christian from the joy and hope that is her rightful inheritance. If you feel broken today, remember that none of us wrestles merely against flesh and blood. Ask the Lord to help you focus on what is true, and find a godly friend who will help you get back into the battle.

The one who states his case first seems right, until the other comes and examines him. The lot puts an end to quarrels and decides between powerful contenders. A brother offended is more unyielding than a strong city, and quarreling is like the bars of a castle.

Proverbs 18:17-19 ESV

In order for genuine justice to be dispensed, both parties in a case must be heard. Although one may passionately insist she is in the right, there are always two sides to every story. The unfair judge rules in one direction before giving full weight to all persons involved. In most quarrels, both sides are somewhat to blame. In the end, God knows who is at fault. Those who are at odds with one another often live as if there were a castle wall between them, foolishly allowing their need to be right to fuel their personal war. But women who trust in the Lord cease from fighting, confident that the same God who showers his people with mercy will make things right in the end. With whom are you at odds? Nothing is more comical to the watching world than brawls between believers. For the sake of the gospel, get over your petty disputes today.

From the fruit of a man's mouth his stomach is satisfied; he is satisfied by the yield of his lips Death and life are in the power of the tongue, and those who love it will eat its fruits.

Proverbs 18:20-21 ESV

The way we use our words determines our level of contentment in life, as what we speak to others will impact us in the end. Just as healthy food makes one well while junk food makes one sickly, so too good words strengthen the soul while bad words corrupt the person. The things we say to people should be the things we expect them to say back to us. Our words have more power than we give them credit for; in fact, they can be the cause of death or of life in our community. Statements we make can cause divisions between people and strife between others and ourselves. The one who speaks encouragement has the ability to bring healing to those around her. We are driven by what others say, and others are driven by what we communicate. It has been said, "You are what you eat," but the Proverbs warn, "You are what you speak."

He who finds a wife finds a good thing and obtains favor from the Lord. The poor use entreaties, but the rich answer roughly. A man of many companions may come to ruin, but there is a friend who sticks closer than a brother.

Proverbs 18:22-24 ESV

If a man is wise, he will seek out a God-fearing wife, and a wise woman will look for a God-fearing husband. Godly character should be the most important trait required when considering a future spouse. Those who are poor have no financial means to turn to for deliverance and are fully dependent upon the Lord for help. The wealthy, on the other hand, often make riches their primary source of security and are harsh with those who ask them to share their resources. Though one may have many friends when circumstances are going well, few friends stick around when disaster strikes. In the end, it's not about the number of friends you have, but about the quality of those friendships. Better to have a faithful friend you can trust with your life than a hundred so-called friends you can't even trust with your reputation.

Better is a poor person who walks in his integrity than one who is crooked in speech and is a fool. Desire without knowledge is not good, and whoever makes haste with his feet misses his way.

Proverbs 19:1-2 ESV

Even though the poor person will encounter difficulty in this life, in the end she will be better off than one who lies and takes advantage of others. Soon, God will punish sin and make all things right. No matter what calamity falls upon the poor person, if her hope is in the Lord, she has more reason for rejoicing than even the wealthiest human on earth. The wicked woman rushes to increase her worldly assets and misses God's desire for her life along the way. If you are feeling discouraged by a lack of finances or any other good thing, remember that God has promised he will never leave or forsake us. The favor God has bestowed upon us now in forgiving our sins will follow us for all eternity. As the pleasures of this life are truly fleeting and momentary, so are the sufferings. Those who keep an eternal perspective live consistent with ultimate reality.

When a man's folly brings his way to ruin, his heart rages against the Lord. Wealth brings many new friends, but a poor man is deserted by his friend.

Proverbs 19:3-4 ESV

The fool makes poor decisions with time, resources, friendships, and hobbies, seeking self-satisfaction rather than humbly and respectfully living according to the wisdom of the Lord. When his plans fail him and he doesn't prosper in self-indulgent folly, his stupidity escalates even further, and he actually blames God for not honoring his careless lifestyle. He doesn't submit himself to the Lord and his law, yet he becomes angry with God for not giving him what he wants. People often gravitate toward the woman with money, hoping to gain financially from the friendship. But those same people want nothing to do with her once she loses her wealth. Those who possess money can be loved as much as money itself. Have you made foolish decisions in life for which you are now suffering the consequences? If so, see your lack of prosperity as a demonstration of God's kindness toward you, that you might repent and realign your life before it's too late.

A false witness will not go unpunished, and he who breathes out lies will not escape. Many seek the favor of a generous man, and everyone is a friend to a man who gives gifts.

Proverbs 19:5-6 ESV

The court should be a place where people administer justice. Those who oversee the legal process depend upon witnesses to give testimony by accurately communicating what they experienced or know regarding a given case. But not all witnesses are truth tellers. Although they may prosper before man, even within the judicial system, God knows all and will not leave liars unpunished. Flattery is used to gain the confidence of the one who is able to rule favorably, and money can ensure a desired verdict. If you are discouraged today because an evil man successfully used flattery or money to pervert justice, don't lose heart. Keep doing the right thing. Not one person will escape the judgment of God. On that day, every human soul will be fully exposed before the One to whom all will give an account. No clever words or stack of cash will manipulate the Lord of the universe.

All a poor man's brothers hate him; how much more do his friends go far from him! He pursues them with words, but does not have them. Whoever gets sense loves his own soul; he who keeps understanding will discover good. A false witness will not go unpunished, and he who breathes out lies will perish.

Proverbs 19:7-9 ESV

As she continually cries out for financial help, the one who is poor can drag down family members. And if she is a burden to her blood relatives, how much more is she a nuisance to those who aren't even related! Even though she may continue to express her needs to friends and family, she gets no help. But the person who earnestly pursues God's wisdom, living in a way that is consistent with the teaching of the Lord, will enjoy abundant life now and eternally. God is aware of everything said by every person. Not a single word or even thought of a word escapes his notice. The one who lies to get out of trouble may experience momentary relief, but she will eventually deal with the consequences of her false testimony. Better to tell the truth and temporarily suffer now than to lie and permanently suffer later.

It is not fitting for a fool to live in luxury, much less for a slave to rule over princes. Good sense makes one slow to anger, and it is his glory to overlook an offense. A king's wrath is like the growling of a lion, but his favor is like dew on the grass.

Proverbs 19:10-12 ESV

When the fool experiences God's goodness, he is driven further from the Lord, thinking the blessings he enjoys are a result of his own clever choices. Abandoning justice, an unwise slave would use power allotted to him for selfish purposes. The godly woman turns from anger, looking beyond her own rights. She reflects the character of the Lord, who has pardoned her sin, punishing his Son on the cross in her place. In contrast, the fury of the king can go unrestrained. Nevertheless, it is wise to seek his favor by living above reproach. To remain in good standing with those in positions of authority provides rest from strife. Every person will be wronged in this life. What do you do when hurt by others? Are you quick to overlook the offense, mindful of the wrongs you have been forgiven, or do you harbor resentment? To keep oneself from unwise anger is glorious.

A foolish son is ruin to his father, and a wife's quarreling is a continual dripping of rain. House and wealth are inherited from fathers, but a prudent wife is from the Lord.

Proverbs 19:13-14 ESV

The father of a foolish son has no one to come alongside him in his old age or to manage the family's wealth. A complaining wife sounds like water dripping from a faulty ceiling. In ancient Israel, rooftops were made of wood and clay, and when a rainstorm struck, leaking would surely follow. The only way for a man to escape the noise was to leave his home. The household must be managed wisely, and a man is dependent upon his wife. Though marriages were arranged at the time, the good wife was a gift from God. If you are married, do you bicker with your husband? If you will be married, are you currently content to yield your desires for the benefit of your other family members? If you have a hard time getting along with family, the problem might be you. Be a godly woman by choosing to look out for the needs of others today.

Slothfulness casts into a deep sleep, and an idle person will suffer hunger. Whoever keeps the commandment keeps his life; he who despises his ways will die.

Proverbs 19:15-16 ESV

The unwise person's laziness causes her to become a sluggard. Her desire for sleep keeps her shut off from the world around her. In time, she becomes unaware of her situation's severity. Like one who is continually intoxicated, her tiredness makes her useless and unproductive. She misses out on life and ends up hungry, empty, and even lonely as a result. The responsible person, on the other hand, keeps the commands of Scripture. By trusting in God and his word, she will live now and eternally. The fool insists that she doesn't care. She is uninterested in disciplining herself for godliness. She will suffer loss now and in the life to come. Although there's nothing wrong with taking breaks and getting time off from our busy schedules, we should never become people who despise work. If you have been in an undisciplined rut, put an end to that today. Get up, get busy, and make a difference!

Whoever is generous to the poor lends to the Lord, and he will repay him for his deed. Discipline your son, for there is hope; do not set your heart on putting him to death. A man of great wrath will pay the penalty, for if you deliver him, you will only have to do it again.

Proverbs 19:17-19 ESV

The person who helps the poor helps the Lord himself. By lending to the less fortunate, the godly woman lends to the Lord, who values all human life. God will repay her for her kindness. The one who oppresses the poor is sure to face the judgment of God. The woman who loves her son will discipline him. Parents who fail to biblically correct their children set them up for eternal death, as loving discipline drives folly from the child. The man with an unreasonable spirit should not be bailed out of his troubles. He must experience the natural consequences of his ungodly behavior. The one who tries to repair circumstances for others often ends up interfering with God's corrective discipline. Does someone in your life continually need you to clean up her mess? If so, maybe it's time to back off and let God work his will in her life. Stay out of the way of the Holy Spirit.

August

Listen to advice and accept instruction, that you may gain wisdom in the future. Many are the plans in the mind of a man, but it is the purpose of the Lord that will stand.

Proverbs 19:20-21 ESV

The father reminds his son of how critical it is that he listen to and put godly advice into practice. By doing so, the son will enjoy the blessing of wisdom, both in this age and the age to come. By acquiring wisdom, the son can face the future with confidence instead of fear. The father goes on to explain why this wisdom is so important. The human mind may make many plans for the future, but in the end, only what God allows will transpire. Even the most carefully thought out intentions will fail before the Lord if they are not part of his providential plan. The wise person trusts that God is working all things together for the good of those who love him. Even in the face of suffering, God can take what was intended for harm and instead bring redemption from the darkness. Those who obey the Lord will ultimately live "happily ever after."

What is desired in a man is steadfast love,
and a poor man is better than a liar.
The fear of the Lord leads to life, and
whoever has it rests satisfied; he will
not be visited by harm. The sluggard
buries his hand in the dish and will not
even bring it back to his mouth.

Proverbs 19:22-24 ESV

We all hope to find someone who will be there for us in our time of need. How devastating it is when the one we trusted lies to us! Better to embrace poverty than to misplace our trust in those who let us down. But those who fear the Lord will never be disappointed. In the end, the wise disciple will not suffer hunger or calamity. In contrast to the godly, the sluggard has no fear of God. She is so lazy that even when she puts her hand into her plate, she decides it's too much work to bring it back to her mouth. Though there are opportunities everywhere, she would rather starve than exercise self-discipline. Are you a sluggard? What about in spiritual matters? Do you do what God has called you to and quickly? Or do you sit around stumped, too lazy to make the changes you should have made yesterday?

Strike a scoffer, and the simple will learn prudence; reprove a man of understanding, and he will gain knowledge. He who does violence to his father and chases away his mother is a son who brings shame and reproach. Cease to hear instruction, my son, and you will stray from the words of knowledge.

Proverbs 19:25-27 ESV

Discipline and punishment are necessary to instruct the one who mocks wisdom. Even those who are simple can gain insight by watching the scoffer face the consequences of his foolish behavior. The wise person responds to good advice, and learns from the mistakes and sound choices of others. The shameful son is an utter embarrassment to his parents and the community. His self-indulgent actions create financial problems for his father, leaving his dependent mother in a state of need. Obsessed with his desires for personal gain, he would go so far as to evict his parents if he could seize their property. The more the son deviates from sound teaching, the more his heart becomes hardened to wisdom. When the mind of the Lord as revealed through his word is not earnestly sought after, spiritual drift will result. The path of wisdom is an uphill course; to remain on it requires hard work and continual effort.

A worthless witness mocks at justice, and the mouth of the wicked devours iniquity. Condemnation is ready for scoffers, and beating for the backs of fools.

Proverbs 19:28-29 ESV

The wicked person seeks to pervert justice. Although she has first-hand knowledge that would be helpful in determining truth, she's not interested in honesty. Instead, she gives false testimony, relishing the injustice that results from her lies. Her mouth swallows evil, and she can't consume it fast enough. Although she enjoys the outcome of her dishonesty, she will face judgment when God makes all things right. The one who refuses to align her desires under the revealed will of God will be punished. The fool will also be beaten because of his poor choices. Though these consequences are not corrective, like the loving discipline that comes from a good father, they can be effective. If you are suffering because of poor decisions, put an end to your foolish behavior. Although you may have to accept the fallout of your sinful choices, you can still determine to submit yourself to God. It's a great day to start all over again.

Wine is a mocker, strong drink a brawler, and whoever is led astray by it is not wise. The terror of a king is like the growling of a lion; whoever provokes him to anger forfeits his life. It is an honor for a man to keep aloof from strife, but every fool will be quarreling

Proverbs 20:1-3 ESV

The one who is drunk loses self-control and ends up making poor decisions which lead to all sorts of ungodly behavior. Only the fool allows herself to become intoxicated by alcohol or any other substance. It is dumb to do anything that would unnecessarily provoke the strong arm of the law. The wise woman avoids strife and conflict. She will often forgo her rights for the sake of peace in the community, while the foolish woman demands that her own needs be met. When you are insulted or overlooked, how do you respond? Do you calmly trust in God's ability to exercise justice, or do you blow your top until your case is heard? What about at home? Would your family members characterize you as a peaceful or an angry person? Make sure there's no gap between who you are in public and in private. The real you is revealed by what you do when no human is watching.

The sluggard does not plow in the autumn; he will seek at harvest and have nothing. The purpose in a man's heart is like deep water, but a man of understanding will draw it out. Many a man proclaims his own steadfast love, but a faithful man who can find?

Proverbs 20:4-6 ESV

In autumn, the ancient farmer needed to work hard, plowing his field early to later yield a harvest and supply his household with food. The sluggard was too lazy to do the dirty work of turning up soil long before seeds could be planted. He didn't want to sweat, but instead expected to enjoy the fruit of someone else's labor. The deceitful man buries self-seeking motives within his heart, thinking none will see why he does what he does. But the wise man is able to discern his schemes. The phony man boasts about how loyal he is, but when the rubber meets the road, it's all about him. What a blessing it is to find a genuine friend who sticks by your side! Do you have a friend like that? If not, determine to be kind to others today. You never know who may end up being faithful to you in return.

*The righteous who walks in his integrity—
blessed are his children after him! A king
who sits on the throne of judgment winnows
all evil with his eyes.*

Proverbs 20:7-8 ESV

Despite the darkness in our world, God has chosen some to walk uprightly before him, trusting in his word and choosing to submit themselves to his laws and principles. These people invest into others and look out for the good of the community. The descendants of the righteous are set apart from those without believing parents; the children of the upright reap the rich benefits of being raised in a God-fearing home. The wise ruler is able to distinguish the wicked from the righteous. He evaluates behavior and even sees through to the motives of those in his kingdom. In justice, he removes those who are evil from his realm. In the end, God alone is able to honestly winnow, or examine, all of humanity. On the last day, we will be found either in Christ or outside of Christ. And in the end, that's all that really matters. Which group would you be found in today?

Who can say, "I have made my heart pure; I am clean from my sin"? Unequal weights and unequal measures are both alike an abomination to the Lord. Even a child makes himself known by his acts, by whether his conduct is pure and upright.

Proverbs 20:9-11 ESV

The wise realize that no human is able to live according to God's holy standard of behavior. No one is good. Although some may be better than others, not one is pure before our perfect God. The Lord demands honesty. Those who use unequal weights and measures deceive others. Ultimately, when we defraud each another, we attempt to deceive God, but that's not going to happen. When we look at children, it becomes evident that all are born with a corrupt nature. We teach and train our children to do justly, love mercy, and live humbly before God, but left to themselves, our children, like us, are self-absorbed. If you believe that by yourself you are good enough for God, you are wrong. If you have never done so, humble yourself before the Almighty today, casting yourself upon his mercy and trusting in the provision he made for you in the work of Christ on the cross.

The hearing ear and the seeing eye, the Lord has made them both. Love not sleep, lest you come to poverty; open your eyes, and you will have plenty of bread.

Proverbs 20:12-13 ESV

The student of wisdom must listen attentively to the word of the Lord, remaining on the alert with her eye fixed on the path of the righteous. To gain insight, she must hear godly advice and put it into practice. Without the careful work of both listening and observation, she simply will not become wise. The alert eye takes advantage of the opportunities God brings to her, but the lazy eye loves sleep. This lazy woman continually looks for "time off." And as the days and months go by, she ends up empty. Although our sinful nature pulls at us to be spiritually lazy, we must resist its call. We seek God, invest in our families, serve at church, work hard, and rest in order to do it all again. When we labor for Jesus, our work becomes a delight. Work hard today, as if you were serving the very King of Kings, because in the end, you are!

"Bad, bad," says the buyer, but when he goes away, then he boasts. There is gold and abundance of costly stones, but the lips of knowledge are a precious jewel. Take a man's garment when he has put up security for a stranger, and hold it in pledge when he puts up security for foreigners.

Proverbs 20:14-16 ESV

God is not pleased with unjust transactions. We may act like something isn't worth much and then rejoice because of the great "deal" we got, but the Lord does not condone this deceit. If the item is "bad," then why buy it? Expensive things may be worth much, but honest words are most prized. It is stupid to jeopardize your life for the debt of a stranger. The one who puts herself at risk might as well have her own property taken away. Are you willing to be honest, even if it means you may miss the better end of an exchange? Or do you keep silent, later to return home boasting about how you took advantage of someone? If your gain means someone else's loss, then walk away from the deal. You may not end up with a sack of gold, but your character will be worth more than any bank account can buy.

Bread gained by deceit is sweet to a man, but afterward his mouth will be full of gravel. Plans are established by counsel; by wise guidance wage war. Whoever goes about slandering reveals secrets; therefore do not associate with a simple babbler.

Proverbs 20:17-19 ESV

The deceptive woman may enjoy the fruit of her schemes, but in the end the "sweetness" will be gone. She will be left with a mouth full of rocks, which break the teeth, rather than bread, which satisfies the appetite. The godly woman pays attention to advice and receives correction well. Before using any sort of force to overcome enemies, it is wise to get biblical counsel. Only plans consistent with God's desire will succeed. The gossip is known for revealing the latest news and secrets of others. She has the dirt on everyone in the community and even prides herself in how much she knows. But don't be deceived. Just as this woman easily betrays the confidence of others, she's quick to let people in on your secrets too. Avoid the one who consistently "has the scoop" on others. The news you take in isn't at all worth the information about you that's going out.

If one curses his father or his mother, his lamp will be put out in utter darkness. An inheritance gained hastily in the beginning will not be blessed in the end.

Proverbs 20:20-21 ESV

The foolish son insults his mother and father, but God will cause his cursing to turn back upon him. Just as the law teaches that those who honor their parents will live long, those who disparage their parents will be cut off prematurely. Many fathers labor diligently to leave something to their children, but the one who can't wait to get her hands on an inheritance will experience the Lord's punishment. Parents who truly love their children will speak and teach truth. Godly parents don't cower before their children, seeking their approval, but instead recognize that if they don't discipline their kids, God will. Our culture pressures us to worship our children; many even change churches or theology to appease their offspring. Trust God enough to be firm with your kids today. It would be better for you to be rejected by your kids now than for God to reject them later.

Do not say, "I will repay evil"; wait for the Lord, and he will deliver you. Unequal weights are an abomination to the Lord, and false scales are not good.

Proverbs 20:22-23 ESV

God will help the oppressed and righteous woman, taking care of her, while punishing those who bring her harm. When you are wronged and rejected, resist the temptation to get revenge on your own. God is the source of all justice in the universe. He will not allow any transgression to go unpunished. As an earthly father often quietly watches his children and the way they treat one another, so God watches us. But unlike the earthly father, God sees everything, including every motive behind what is done. When a child is mistreated by her siblings, the father will often sit back for a moment and allow the wronged child to develop strength and character. Yet at the perfect time, the father will step in and settle the score. If you have been wronged, know that God sees your plight. He knows exactly what is going on, precisely what he plans to do, and he will make everything right in the end.

A man's steps are from the Lord; how then can man understand his way? It is a snare to say rashly, "It is holy," and to reflect only after making vows.

Proverbs 20:24-25 ESV

Although unjust things occur, those who trust in the Lord do not need to live in fear, since God is sovereign over all the ways of mankind. As creatures, humans will never outwit the Lord. People strategize and step forward, but God supersedes man's plans. Wisdom advises against making quick vows regarding what we will and won't do for the kingdom of God. The woman who serves habitually, without resorting to impulsive resolutions, lives balanced and with less regret. This wise woman looks to the Lord rather than others, including herself, to work everything together for his good. All are responsible for the decisions they make, and yet God determines how the affairs of men will end. You can push and plan all you want, but if God opposes your demands, they aren't going to happen. The godly woman yields all, including her hopes, desires, and dreams, to the Lord's faithful care.

A wise king winnows the wicked and drives the wheel over them. The spirit of man is the lamp of the Lord, searching all his innermost parts. Steadfast love and faithfulness preserve the king, and by steadfast love his throne is upheld.

Proverbs 20:26-28 ESV

Just as the wheel of a cart is driven over plucked heads of grain to thoroughly divide them, rulers use godly wisdom to distinguish between the righteous and the wicked, eliminating evil from their realm. God is aware of all that goes on in the universe, and we will face full and honest judgment when we stand before his throne. The good king, though unable to see men's motives, seeks to uphold the cause of the oppressed. When the king is determined to stand up for justice, he acts on the Lord's behalf. It's easy to forget that God knows everything about us. He even knows how we would behave if given different circumstances. Do you think that if things were different you would be a better person? God already knows how you would act in every possible scenario. God has us exactly where we are today for a very good reason.

The glory of young men is their strength, but the splendor of old men is their gray hair. Blows that wound cleanse away evil; strokes make clean the innermost parts.

Proverbs 20:29-30 ESV

There are benefits to both youth and age. The young have more physical strength and energy than the aged, but those who are mature possess the wisdom that comes from years and decades of righteous living. The youth and the elderly complement one another and should see their need for dependence upon each other. When wrong behavior is met with painful consequences, the suffering that results can work like the external scrubbing of metal pots to cleanse from impurity. Though no one enjoys being hurt, the blows of life can add to a person's integrity, strength, and ability to navigate circumstances in a godly manner. In age, are you young or old? If you are old, are you sharing wisdom with the youth around you? And if you are young, are you purposefully seeking out older mentors? Don't isolate yourself from people in different life stages. Work together with one another today.

The king's heart is a stream of water in the hand of the Lord; he turns it wherever he will. Every way of a man is right in his own eyes, but the Lord weighs the heart. To do righteousness and justice is more acceptable to the Lord than sacrifice.

Proverbs 21:1-3 ESV

Just as a farmer directs water by digging trenches, so the Lord guides the affairs of men. The king is the most powerful of all, believing he can do whatever he wants, and yet God is in control of the king's wishes. The Lord uses the king to provide for his people. One may believe her motives are right, but God sees everything. Though it is proper to give to God what he is due, the Lord prefers internal obedience to external service. God expects our visible display of devotion to mirror our inward commitment to him. No matter how free we may feel, we must humbly acknowledge that everything we have comes from God. Even if your longings are good and right, you owe that to the Lord. Pray that God would make your desires consistent with his today. He can, and he will do so for those who ask.

Haughty eyes and a proud heart, the lamp of the wicked, are sin. The plans of the diligent lead surely to abundance, but everyone who is hasty comes only to poverty.

Proverbs 21:4-5 ESV

Those who are obsessed with themselves look down on others with haughty eyes. They are quick to criticize, and they ignorantly believe they are superior to people around them. Their egotism is rooted in the core of their being. The proud see no real need to submit their desires under God's demands. In fact, they believe the Lord will ultimately embrace their beliefs regarding proper behavior. God will "discover" that they were right. What fools! Those who scheme to get a fast dollar lose out on what is truly valuable in life. The hard working and righteous woman will be rewarded in the end. Her labor and care in managing her resources will yield unexpected profits. Do you habitually compare yourself with others? We should evaluate ourselves before God, not people. When we admit our moral failure before a holy God, we lose our arrogant attitudes, we live humbly, and we replace criticism with compassion.

The getting of treasures by a lying tongue is a fleeting vapor and a snare of death. The violence of the wicked will sweep them away, because they refuse to do what is just. The way of the guilty is crooked, but the conduct of the pure is upright.

Proverbs 21:6-8 ESV

Those who gain wealth by deception will be rewarded with emptiness. They lie to get what they want, but are never satisfied. Although they oppress, even by violence, in the end, they will be destroyed. They are like fish caught in a net, soon dragged away to certain death. Even though they have opportunity to repent, they aren't interested. They fight God to the very end, refusing to trust him with their lives. They have no interest in the straight path which seems boring, insisting that God's way would strip the fun from their lives. They resist the testimony of their conscience, the Spirit, and God's word, thinking they will worm their way out of personal responsibility in the judgment. In contrast, the upright, who have turned from living for self to following the way of the Lord, are made blameless. Because the righteous put their trust in the Lord, he will keep them pure to the very end.

It is better to live in a corner of the housetop than in a house shared with a quarrelsome wife. The soul of the wicked desires evil; his neighbor finds no mercy in his eyes.

Proverbs 21:9-10 ESV

Living with a roof over our heads should be a reason for rejoicing, but not so for the man with a quarrelsome wife. He would be better off sleeping alone on his rooftop, exposed to heat, wind, and rain, than stuck inside with a nagging woman. The aggressive woman thinks continually about herself. She is not content until she gets her way. Even when she keeps her mouth shut, she invents clever methods to manipulate those around her. The core of the wicked person's being corrupts her desires, causing her to seek out evil. According to this woman, no one is worthy of mercy. She refuses kindness to her neighbor and brings harm to those near her. Both the quarrelsome wife and the evil neighbor are passionate about themselves. What about you? Are you a nag? Do you push and push until you get your way? Or is your soul quiet within you, resting in the protection and provision of the Lord?

When a scoffer is punished, the simple becomes wise; when a wise man is instructed, he gains knowledge. The Righteous One observes the house of the wicked; he throws the wicked down to ruin.

Proverbs 21:11-12 ESV

The mocker learns that when she disobeys God and his commands, she experiences his discipline, and in time she can actually become wise, making better choices. Once she acquires wisdom, she habitually listens to and applies godly advice to her thinking and actions. She realizes that there is great benefit in obeying the Lord. His commandments are a blessing and not a burden. God is aware of every action and every thought of every person. He is the Righteous One and will overthrow the wicked, ultimately removing them from his presence. Where would you be found with respect to wisdom today? Are you the scoffer who resists the revealed word of God, thinking that your way is better than his? Or are you wise, recognizing that the Lord has given us his law to keep us from a life of regrets? The wise woman eagerly anticipates every opportunity to align her life with God's design for human behavior.

Whoever closes his ear to the cry of the poor will himself call out and not be answered. A gift in secret averts anger, and a concealed bribe, strong wrath. When justice is done, it is a joy to the righteous but terror to evildoers.

Proverbs 21:13-15 ESV

The helpless repeatedly cry out to those with resources, but the wicked woman ignores their pleas. When the hardhearted woman is thrust into her hour of need, there will be none to rescue her. The destitute are unable to bribe people in high places. Although the calloused woman turns her back to the cries of the helpless, she bends to the one bearing gifts. This must be done in secret, as even the evil recognize bribery as a perversion of justice. One day, all will give account to God, and transgressors of his law will be punished. Jesus taught us to do for others as we would like them to do for us. Think about how you would like to be treated. What would bring joy in the midst of the struggles you are currently facing? Now think of someone to whom you could bring the same relief. Follow up by putting that last thought into action today.

One who wanders from the way of good sense will rest in the assembly of the dead. Whoever loves pleasure will be a poor man; he who loves wine and oil will not be rich. The wicked is a ransom for the righteous, and the traitor for the upright.

Proverbs 21:16-18 ESV

Those who turn from wisdom, thinking they can find an easier path, will end up rejected by God. Ironically, in their attempt to gain worldly rest they forfeit eternal rest. If a woman compromises truth to obtain satisfaction, she should recognize that the price tag associated with the temporary pleasures of this life is too high. The one who longs for enjoyment now engulfed in the present age will discover that she missed opportunities to lay up an eternal reward. Wine and oil represent the good life. Wine is associated with feasting and enjoying wonderful foods, and oil is refreshing and medicinal to the body. There is nothing wrong with treasuring the blessings God has graced us with, but when we make the blessings our priority, we miss out on God's design. Appreciate all that God has given you today, but be sure to enjoy your relationship with him even more.

It is better to live in a desert land than with a quarrelsome and fretful woman. Precious treasure and oil are in a wise man's dwelling, but a foolish man devours it.

Proverbs 21:19-20 ESV

Previously, the Proverbs cautioned that a man would be better on his roof than in his home with a quarrelsome woman. Now the Proverbs add more to the warning. Although the desert is uncomfortable, lonely, and even dangerous, a solitary existence in the wasteland is preferable to living with a quarrelsome woman. The fretful woman stirs up trouble in her home. She is constantly worried about tomorrow and attempts to control her husband and her circumstances. No wonder her husband would be better off looking for a rock to hide under. In contrast, the dwelling of the wise man abounds with food, trust, and peace. But given to a fool, the best circumstances are quickly gulped down and selfishly consumed. Are you a fretful woman? Do you stress out about what will happen tomorrow, next week, or even next year? If anxiety plagues you, why not follow the advice of Jesus by focusing on this day? Resist any futile desire to control the future.

Whoever pursues righteousness and kindness will find life, righteousness, and honor. A wise man scales the city of the mighty and brings down the stronghold in which they trust. Whoever keeps his mouth and his tongue keeps himself out of trouble.

Proverbs 21:21-23 ESV

The Lord grants those who seek after righteousness and kindness the blessings of a godly life. The wise person overpowers the wicked. Although evil women may feel safe and even protected by a strong city wall, the wicked are conquered by the wise woman's virtuous behavior. Those who have God on their side may suffer temporarily, but will eventually prevail over all their enemies. One way the righteous woman avoids the traps of the wicked is by guarding what comes out of her own mouth. The woman who cautiously considers what she says, not driven by impulsive rage, but instead thoughtful, will protect herself from trouble. Although some may insist on letting everyone know what's on their minds when angry, doing so is never wise. Think before you speak. Many have destroyed opportunities for future prosperity by blurting out careless words.

"Scoffer" is the name of the arrogant, haughty man who acts with arrogant pride. The desire of the sluggard kills him, for his hands refuse to labor. All day long he craves and craves, but the righteous gives and does not hold back.

Proverbs 21:24-26 ESV

The one who mocks is saturated with pride. Her over-inflated opinion of self causes her to resist and lash out against God and others. She believes she knows more than God and would never be found seeking the counsel of his word. Although the sluggard wants material goods, she is too lazy to work. The desire for food and resources, which drives the normal person to labor and self-sacrifice, frustrates the lazy woman, and she lives with unmet longings. Everything the sluggard ends up getting is spent on herself. The righteous woman stands in contrast to the lazy. The upright woman seeks to meet the desires of others, and will be blessed herself. The arrogant woman has no desire for the Lord, looking down on those who acknowledge their need for salvation. Do you admit you need God's help? Or are you self-righteous, trusting your own works will be sufficient when you stand before his throne?

The sacrifice of the wicked is an abomination; how much more when he brings it with evil intent. A false witness will perish, but the word of a man who hears will endure. A wicked man puts on a bold face, but the upright gives thought to his ways.

Proverbs 21:27-29 ESV

God refuses the one who brings him a sacrifice and yet has never done as he commands by turning from sin and trusting in his provision. Even more so, God rejects the one who uses his name for selfish reasons. The one who gives false testimony will face God's judgment, but the word of the honest witness will endure. The wicked woman becomes shameless in her efforts to deceive. She reaches the point of brazen manipulation of others. The righteous one considers her own actions and motives. Sadly, there will always be those among God's people who appear with us, yet are inwardly using the Lord and his followers for personal gain. These wicked people view the members of the church as potential dollar signs, and seek to gain a reputation for godliness in order to prey upon the good graces of others. Avoid these people the same way God does.

No wisdom, no understanding, no counsel can avail against the Lord. The horse is made ready for the day of battle, but the victory belongs to the Lord.

Proverbs 21:30-31 ESV

Even the best human wisdom, understanding, and advice cannot stand against the will of the Lord. No man or woman can contend with the omniscience and omnipotence of God. Men may employ horses or whatever other means they rely on for power and might, but in the end, even the most deadly of human weapons falls like dust before the Almighty. Although the ungodly may live in defiance of the Lord and reject his authority, none can escape his sovereign control. It was common in the ancient near east to put one's confidence in the size of his army. But no army will ever prevail against God's predetermined plan. In what are you tempted to put your confidence? Is it your bank account, your health and beauty, your intelligence, your family, or your friends? None of these things can save you in the end. All can and will be taken as the Lord wills.

A good name is to be chosen rather than great riches, and favor is better than silver or gold. The rich and the poor meet together; the Lord is the maker of them all.

Proverbs 22:1-2 ESV

Although it is a blessing to have material wealth, and God graces those who walk uprightly with what they need, even more desired than finances is a good reputation. A person's standing in the community often reveals character. Those who walk uprightly are generally well thought of, while those who live in a self-seeking fashion are usually frowned upon by neighbors. Both the rich and the poor bear the image of God, and both are equally valuable to him. God does not show favoritism. You may look down on the less fortunate in your midst and even wince when crossing paths with the extremely poor, but God sees differently. What kind of reputation do you have in your communities? Are you respected, or are you known for being egotistic and insensitive? Do what you can to maintain a good name among those around you, which usually begins by putting others before yourself.

The prudent sees danger and hides himself, but the simple go on and suffer for it. The reward for humility and fear of the Lord is riches and honor and life. Thorns and snares are in the way of the crooked; whoever guards his soul will keep far from them.

Proverbs 22:3-5 ESV

The wise exercise thoughtful discernment. They keep themselves from the consequences of evil by avoiding sinful behavior and staying clear of those who would lure them into darkness. The foolish carelessly charge on in the face of danger and suffer for it. Those who fear the Lord are humble. They recognize their need for God's moral compass and diligently follow after his word. The simple scoff at God's laws; they think the best course of action for life lies in living independent of God's revealed will. Whatever benefit the unwise enjoy in life is temporary, but the gains of those who are right with the Lord carry on into the life to come. The crooked man seeks after whatever sparkles. He grabs at the chance for fast sex and quick money. He thinks he's on top of the world, but in no time will crash to the ground. Avoid the traps and enticements of evil behavior at all costs. The moral price tag is unaffordable.

Train up a child in the way he should go; even when he is old he will not depart from it. The rich rules over the poor, and the borrower is the slave of the lender. Whoever sows injustice will reap calamity, and the rod of his fury will fail.

Proverbs 22:6-8 ESV

It is critical that one stay on the right road, and so the Proverbs exhort parents to instruct their children to follow the way of wisdom from the beginning of life. The rich person has plenty and enjoys stress-free circumstances, while those who are poor end up trapped in financial slavery, paying interest they can't afford. The Lord, who sees all, will judge those who selfishly abuse their power and wealth. When people walk along a specific path, the ground beneath them becomes hard, and over time a trench forms. As the path gets more and more use, the trench becomes deeper and deeper and less easy to deviate from. It is the same with moral training. Do everything you can to work godly habits into your kids at a young age. The courses paved in childhood have a lasting impact on adult life, even into old age.

Whoever has a bountiful eye will be blessed, for he shares his bread with the poor. Drive out a scoffer, and strife will go out, and quarreling and abuse will cease. He who loves purity of heart, and whose speech is gracious, will have the king as his friend.

Proverbs 22:9-11 ESV

The generous woman shares her resources with those less fortunate. Even the food she has allotted to herself and her family is further divided to help the poor. Though she may not be wealthy, she still gives to others without expecting anything in return. The unrepentant mocker must be banished to protect the integrity of the community. The person who is right with the Lord, evidenced by selfless and kind speech, has access to the ear of the king. The wise person is able to rule her tongue. She is trustworthy, honest, gives good advice, and keeps from damaging others with careless and harmful words. Although it's been said that only "sticks and stones break bones," the Proverbs repeatedly warn that words can and do hurt, often causing long-term suffering. If you have been foolish with your speech, repent today, and ask the Lord to help you carefully monitor what comes from your mouth.

The eyes of the Lord keep watch over knowledge, but he overthrows the words of the traitor. The sluggard says, "There is a lion outside! I shall be killed in the streets!" The mouth of forbidden women is a deep pit; he with whom the Lord is angry will fall into it.

Proverbs 22:12-14 ESV

God's word will stand to the end. The Lord protects knowledge and derails unfaithful speech. The sluggard speaks lies to justify his laziness. He claims that although he wants to work, he simply can't, as there is a lion in the streets. To protect himself from potential harm, he must remain home and continue to be provided for by others. The lazy person will fabricate any excuse to keep from buckling down and working hard. The unfaithful woman also speaks lies. She seeks to entice the simple into her trap. In contrast to the fantasy lion in the street, the adulteress is a true danger. She uses flattery and deceptive speech to make naïve men feel self-confident, plunging recklessly into death together with her. The man who gives in will lose everything. Be on guard against deceptive words. Don't use them to avoid hard work, and don't succumb to them when they make you feel good.

Folly is bound up in the heart of a child, but the rod of discipline drives it far from him. Whoever oppresses the poor to increase his own wealth, or gives to the rich, will only come to poverty.

Proverbs 22:15-16 ESV

We all come into this world as self-centered and foolish creatures. We must be trained to resist our sinful desires and instead make wise decisions. Godly parents will teach their children to do so, employing painful consequences when the child makes dangerous decisions. The Lord will judge those who take from or overwork the poor only to lavish goods upon the rich. Make sure you aren't favoring the elite while overlooking the less fortunate. Just as loving parents discipline their children, God disciplines his kids. Like the loving parents, God corrects our behavior, often allowing painful consequences for our good, that we would be more like Jesus. Is the Lord correcting you right now? If so, don't resist his instructive ways, but yield to them so that you might become wise. Instead of running from his correction, turn around and embrace the changes he wants you to make. Don't delay your own spiritual growth for another day.

Incline your ear, and hear the words of the wise, and apply your heart to my knowledge, for it will be pleasant if you keep them within you, if all of them are ready on your lips.

Proverbs 22:17-18 ESV

This is the first of thirty explicit sayings. To be wise, one must choose to first listen to sound advice. But merely hearing godly wisdom is not sufficient. The student must also put the truths she learns into practice. In addition, one should memorize the words of the Lord so that biblical instruction saturates her heart and mind, overflowing into the very words she speaks. Though it is hard work to memorize Scripture, it is well worth it. We all commit to memory the things that are important to us. Retained addresses and directions, birthdays and special events, or lines from our favorite movies and songs remind us that we all have the ability to recollect the information that interests us. How much Scripture have you memorized recently? What can you do to add to the amount of biblical wisdom in your mind and heart before the end of this year? Why not begin by memorizing this passage from the Proverbs today!

That your trust may be in the Lord, I
have made them known to you today,
even to you. Have I not written for
you thirty sayings of counsel and
knowledge, to make you know what
is right and true, that you may give
a true answer to those who sent you?

Proverbs 22:19-21 ESV

Although the Proverbs instruct the hearer to walk along the path of righteousness, their primary function is to lead the willing to repentance and faith in God and his Son, Jesus. This advice continues the first of the thirty sayings, which reveal that the father is not random in the advice he imparts, but instead, he has a specific block of instruction available for his son, possibly mirroring an esteemed document of ancient Egyptian wisdom. After learning the wisdom afforded him, the son can give reliable responses to those who ask. In the same way, God has disclosed specific information to us through his word, commanding all to hear and apply his truth. Do you seek the wisdom God has revealed? When you hear the word of the Lord, do you believe it enough to put it into practice? Or do you only obey the parts that seem right to you? Do you believe in God, or yourself?

Do not rob the poor, because he is poor, or crush the afflicted at the gate, for the Lord will plead their cause and rob of life those who rob them.

Proverbs 22:22-23 ESV

Saying 2 explains that in the ancient Near East, the city's gate was where cases were heard and tried by the leaders of the community. The destitute counted upon the kindness of their more affluent neighbors, yet were often taken advantage of, swindled and even robbed by wicked men. The poor could not legally protect themselves from financial exploitation, and those who were sick needed the righteous to advocate for them in court. Those who take advantage of others may think they are getting away with it, but they forget that God stands up for the oppressed. The Lord himself will plead their case. The one who takes from the impoverished will have his very life taken by God. Even though our court systems may fail at times, God keeps a flawless record of all injustice. Don't worry about getting revenge. Instead, entrust yourself to the one who judges justly. In the end, he will make sure that you aren't ripped off.

Make no friendship with a man given to anger, nor go with a wrathful man, lest you learn his ways and entangle yourself in a snare.

Proverbs 22:24-25 ESV

The woman who is easily provoked becomes enraged about relatively unimportant things, ends up making foolish decisions in her moment of passion, and is described in Saying 3. The wrathful woman is easily set off by inconvenient circumstances. Her inner person burns with fury. When she is put out, she makes sure that someone pays for it. The wise woman should not hang out with the one prone to anger. The thoughts and ways of the heated woman are contagious, and she spreads her discontented attitude to those with whom she associates. When her bitter ways infect those around her, they too become caught in a trap of dissatisfaction. How do you respond when things don't go the way you hoped or planned? Do you get frustrated and angry, or do you trust in God's providence to guide the details of your life? Remember, God is in control, and you're not. If you believe that, then live like it.

September
14

Be not one of those who give pledges, who put up security for debts. If you have nothing with which to pay, why should your bed be taken from under you?

Proverbs 22:26-27 ESV

Saying 4 warns against the foolishness of putting up security for the debts of others. It is unwise to get yourself entangled in someone else's financial problems. Although we should be quick to give to and assist those less fortunate, at the same time, to willingly take on another's debt, especially if we cannot afford to just cover it ourselves, is unwise. Why should you worry about whether or not the other party is making her payments? And what happens if she fails to follow through on the commitment? Then you lose the wealth you may have as a result, even down to your own bed. And how have you really helped the one you co-signed for? All you did was enable her to access something she really couldn't afford. Better to help others get work and manage their money properly than to take their financial problems on yourself.

Do not move the ancient landmark that your fathers have set. Do you see a man skillful in his work? He will stand before kings; he will not stand before obscure men.

Proverbs 22:28-29 ESV

Saying 5 reflects the time under Joshua's leadership when the land was divided up and allotted out to the tribes of Israel. Stone landmarks were established to define where private property boundaries existed. Thieves would slowly move the markers so that their own land was increased, while diminishing the property of their neighbors. This practice was equivalent to theft. In Saying 6, the wise son is exhorted to watch for the skilled person, who consistently does the best job he possibly can. Because of his discipline, dedication, and attention to detail, this person will win a good reputation and financial success. How do you work when no one is watching? Do you cut corners and do only as much as needed to get by? Our attitude toward work reflects our respect for God. Whether big tasks, small chores, or even routine homework, choose to do all that you are called to with excellence today.

When you sit down to eat with a ruler, observe carefully what is before you, and put a knife to your throat if you are given to appetite. Do not desire his delicacies, for they are deceptive food.

Proverbs 23:1-3 ESV

Those who are wise realize that careful consideration must be given to every circumstance and opportunity. Saying 7 explains that when dining with someone in authority, the way one conducts herself can make or break her future career. Be thoughtful and restrained in your conversation, use good manners, and by all means, don't order the most expensive thing on the menu! Observing someone in a social setting, such as dining, often reveals more about the person than an interview over a desk. If you can't control your appetites, then don't eat at all. If you are given to drunkenness, don't drink a sip. Avoid anything that would lead you to excess and sin. Don't be deceived, and don't let your guard down. Be sober-minded and thoughtful in all you do. You never know who is watching your level of indulgence or restraint in the things put before you.

Do not toil to acquire wealth; be discerning enough to desist. When your eyes light on it, it is gone, for suddenly it sprouts wings, flying like an eagle toward heaven.

Proverbs 23:4-5 ESV

Saying 8 warns against the pursuit of financial gain independently of God's wisdom. We tend to put our trust in our riches, and the woman who amasses wealth often hopes in her bank account instead of the Lord. When wealth is viewed through the wisdom of Scripture, it can be enjoyed, shared, and even released. The one who is secure in the Lord uses her finances in a way that brings glory to God and the gospel. On the other hand, money is like a powerful eagle who flies through the heavens with none to thwart his course or capture him. When he is ready to depart, he goes, and there is no way to bring him back. In the same way, finances disappear quickly. The one who is foolish can blow through a week's wage in a night or two. And once the money is gone, there's no way to get it back. Find your security in God instead of your wallet.

Do not eat the bread of a man who is stingy; do not desire his delicacies, for he is like one who is inwardly calculating. "Eat and drink!" he says to you, but his heart is not with you. You will vomit up the morsels that you have eaten, and waste your pleasant words.

Proverbs 23:6-8 ESV

According to Saying 9, it's never wise to invite yourself to eat at another's expense, especially if your host is stingy. The tightfisted person who is anxiously seeking to get rich will view your meal in terms of her dollars and cents. To appear hospitable, she may encourage you to dine at her table, but inwardly she despises you and every bite that you take. Even if she offers fine food and drink, exercise wisdom by restraining yourself. Your compliments and words of gratitude will be useless as you praise the one who inwardly detests you and your appetite. Learn self-control by paying for what you consume with your own resources. Be kind to the greedy woman, but refrain from indulging in anything that may cause her to abhor you. Keep your behavior honorable, so that when you are spoken against later, no one will have anything negative to say about you or the God you serve.

*Do not speak in the hearing of a fool,
for he will despise the good sense of your
words. Do not move an ancient landmark
or enter the fields of the fatherless, for
their Redeemer is strong; he will plead
their cause against you.*

Proverbs 23:9-11 ESV

Saying 10 teaches that it's a waste of time to try and engage in intelligent conversation with a fool. The wise person assesses whether or not the one she is speaking with is capable of sensible dialogue before she proceeds to talk about the truths of the Lord. According to Saying 11, the greedy may try and take financial advantage of those who are weak in the community, but the ancient boundaries lines that were established by God are not to be tampered with. God cares about the security of those who don't have adequate protection, and when necessary he will personally punish those who oppress the needy. If you are being taken advantage of, do what you can to right the wrongs you are experiencing, knowing that God stands against those who mistreat the weak. If you want to be like the Lord, extend help to those who are less fortunate in your community today.

Apply your heart to instruction and your ear to words of knowledge. Do not withhold discipline from a child; if you strike him with a rod, he will not die. If you strike him with the rod, you will save his soul from Sheol.

Proverbs 23:12-14 ESV

Saying 12 and the whole of Proverbs remind us that the heart and the ear work together. The ear is for hearing and paying attention to wisdom, while the heart is for putting into practice learned truth. Saying 13 teaches the father to instruct his son that he must discipline his own children. When a child is disobedient, the wise son, acting now as a godly father, must punish wrongdoing. To withhold painful discipline from a child is wicked. Though abuse, including fits of rage and exploding in anger, is unacceptable and sinful, we must never shy away from loving correction when it comes to parenting our children. The wise person leans upon the Lord rather than her own understanding. We can think that because we agree with biblical truth, we are on the path of righteousness. But the wise father repeatedly taught his son that the correct response to God's word requires both listening to and obeying the commands of Scripture.

My son, if your heart is wise, my heart too will be glad. My inmost being will exult when your lips speak what is right.

Proverbs 23:15-16 ESV

Saying 14 reveals that when a child applies God's wisdom to his life, righteous parents rejoice. Parents who fear the Lord yearn for the their children to live according to the word of the Lord. In fact, nothing makes a Christian parent happier than to hear that her children are walking in the truth. The same is true for those who mentor others in the church. Men and women who genuinely love the family of God are overjoyed when they learn that those they have discipled are carefully following after and applying Scripture's wisdom to their lives. When the godly parent hears her offspring speaking and living the word of the Lord, her heart is overwhelmed with gratitude. What are you teaching your children to value? Money and career? Looks and health? Or godly character? In the end, finances and fitness are fleeting, but the one who pursues righteousness will endure to the end.

Let not your heart envy sinners, but continue in the fear of the Lord all the day. Surely there is a future, and your hope will not be cut off.

Proverbs 23:17-18 ESV

The wise, according to Saying 15, are instructed to refrain from passionately longing for what sinners have, and instead keep the fear of the Lord as their focus. The one who consistently makes decisions motivated by a reverential awe of God and his authority will live eternally. In the future, God will wrap up this era of man living on earth and call all to account in judgment. Those who rejected the Lord and mistreated his people will experience his wrath, while those who placed their trust in him, patiently waiting upon him and doing what is right, will be blessed beyond measure. If you see the temporary prosperity of the wicked around you and wonder why things seem to go so well for them, don't forget their end. It is senseless to envy the ease of the ungodly. When you fix your eyes on heaven, the apparent unfairness of this life quickly dims.

Hear, my son, and be wise, and direct your heart in the way. Be not among drunkards or among gluttonous eaters of meat, for the drunkard and the glutton will come to poverty, and slumber will clothe them with rags.

Proverbs 23:19-21 ESV

In Saying 16, the father calls his son to gain wisdom by hearing, following, and keeping his good advice. The son would be foolish to reject the loving parental guidance of his godly father for the wicked ways of sinners. Self-indulgent gluttons and those addicted to wine squander the resources they've been given for immediate, temporary pleasure. The drunkard and the one who eats without restraint will consume her resources until she is left with nothing. Instead of clothing and bedding, the self-indulgent woman will be left with rags for warmth and covering. We live in a world that works hard to convince us we need to purchase more to be happy. But in the end, only our relationship with the Lord will satisfy our souls. Ask God to help you exercise self-discipline today, and say "no" to yourself more often. You really don't need everything you want.

Listen to your father who gave you life,
and do not despise your mother when she
is old. Buy truth, and do not sell it; buy
wisdom, instruction, and understanding.

Proverbs 23:22-23 ESV

The wise son of Saying 17 will humbly take advice from both parents throughout the duration of his life. Although the son's relationship with his mother and father will change as he transitions from a dependent child to an independent adult, he should respect his parents and adhere to the godly wisdom they impart to him. From birth, when the father gives him life, to later days, when his mother is old, the righteous son treats his parents with deferential honor. The wise son will do whatever he can to extract as much wisdom as possible from his upright family, and he will never compromise truth, no matter how appealing the offer. Whether the opportunity involves finances, power, or indulgence, there is nothing more valuable than the wisdom that leads a godly person along the path of the righteous. No short-term pleasure is worth the high price tag associated with sin and disobedience.

The father of the righteous will greatly rejoice; he who fathers a wise son will be glad in him. Let your father and mother be glad; let her who bore you rejoice. My son, give me your heart, and let your eyes observe my ways.

Proverbs 23:24-26 ESV

Saying 17 adds that a wise son brings gladness to his parents. The father and mother of a righteous man rejoice together as they enjoy the blessings that result from their commitment to biblical teaching and training. The whole family benefits from a child's obedience. Saying 18 reveals that the father is entrusted with the welfare of his son, and the son must depend upon his parents' godly wisdom. As the son grows, he is tempted to keep his heart to himself, without accountability. The honorable son gives himself to the care and protection of his upright father. His parents have traveled along the path of the righteous and know what it takes to remain steadfast despite the many obstacles that will appear along the way. Ultimately, the son must give his heart to his heavenly Father. In the same way, as we hand our hopes, dreams, and desires over to the Lord, we can be confident we will be kept safe, now and eternally.

> *For a prostitute is a deep pit; an adulteress is a narrow well. She lies in wait like a robber and increases the traitors among mankind.*

Proverbs 23:27-28 ESV

Saying 18 continues with the righteous son who must place his eyes and his heart in the hands of his father's wise counsel, ultimately entrusting his desires to the authority of the Lord and his word. The immoral woman is on the prowl for any who may be willing to veer from the path of righteousness, and so the son must choose to trust his father's wisdom when confronted with sinful passion. The corrupt woman uses flattery and seductive words to snare her naïve victim into her bed. He doesn't realize that she is manipulating his emotions to fulfill her selfish desires. His passions may conflict with God's wisdom, and if he falls into her trap, there is no escape. It is the same for those who indulge in anything outside of God's parameters for human behavior. Before you step ahead into the next relationship, ask God to show you the cost involved. Your soul will suffer the consequences of your foolish choices.

Who has woe? Who has sorrow? Who has strife? Who has complaining? Who has wounds without cause? Who has redness of eyes? Those who tarry long over wine; those who go to try mixed wine. Do not look at wine when it is red, when it sparkles in the cup and goes down smoothly. In the end it bites like a serpent and stings like an adder.

Proverbs 23:29-32 ESV

The sinful woman of Saying 19 seduces her prey the same way wine lures its victims. Like an immoral woman, wine sparkles in the cup and goes down smoothly. The one who drinks much, tarrying long over wine, is left with emotional pain, relational strife, even physical consequences, such as bloodshot eyes and bruises from a drunken brawl. Though wine may look and even taste good, it has the potential to ruin lives. The good father warns his wise son about the dangers associated with alcohol, advising him to reject any fascination with wine. Alcohol is addictive. Many foolish choices, unwise decisions, and negative, life-altering experiences have resulted from drinking alcohol. Like a snake, even a poisonous snake, alcohol conceals its deadly power in beautiful beverages, but when the drinker gets too close, spending too much time with the bottle, the bite proves deadly. When using alcohol, exercise extreme caution, or avoid it all together.

September
28

Your eyes will see strange things, and your heart utter perverse things. You will be like one who lies down in the midst of the sea, like one who lies on the top of a mast. "They struck me," you will say, "but I was not hurt; they beat me, but I did not feel it. When shall I awake? I must have another drink."

Proverbs 23:33-35 ESV

The father continues his warning in Saying 19 about the dangers associated with drinking alcohol, explaining to his son what will happen if he becomes controlled by wine. Upon intoxication, the son will see and perceive in a way that is inconsistent with reality, even speaking things that simply aren't true. When one becomes inebriated, things turn upside down. Right becomes wrong, and wrong seems right. The drunk begins to wobble and lose his balance as if he were being tossed around like a ship on the sea. The drunk then declares that even though he was beaten, it didn't hurt. Instead of protecting himself, he becomes the town punching bag. Although not all who drink end up physically abused, they are often emotionally or financially beaten, allowing themselves to be exploited by those who take advantage of their intoxicated state. They spend more, say more, and support more than they ever would without the wine. Surprisingly, they return to the bottle again and again.

Be not envious of evil men, nor desire to be with them, for their hearts devise violence, and their lips talk of trouble.

Proverbs 24:1-2 ESV

As we look at the world system around us, we often wonder why the ungodly seem to prosper, while the righteous suffer. Saying 20 warns the wise against any enticement she may feel to entertain these thoughts, cautioning the upright to reject the company of the wicked. The ungodly are egocentric, looking out for their own selfish interests rather than focusing on what would benefit others. They talk about what they want and how they will get it. Whether it be taking someone's resources, reputation, or life, the wicked don't care what happens to anyone else as long as they are temporarily satisfied. But judgment is coming. When they stand before the throne of the King and give an account of their behavior, it will be too late to turn back. Wanting what those who are evil have is foolish. Walk away from any temptation to follow darkness in your actions or your attitude.

> *By wisdom a house is built, and by understanding it is established; by knowledge the rooms are filled with all precious and pleasant riches.*

Proverbs 24:3-4 ESV

There is nothing wrong with enjoying financial blessings in this life, but they must be sought after and kept with a godly attitude. According to Saying 21, the righteous person gains wealth by employing biblical wisdom. She works hard, spends wisely, gives to others, and is satisfied with the resources God has given her. She doesn't envy and chase after everything the world insists that she needs, but maintains a healthy balance between what she buys, what she saves, and what she shares. As she walks along the path of the righteous, her home is filled with good things, including material resources and spiritual blessings. We are bombarded with messages telling us we need to buy, implying that if we just purchase, we will be happier. But that's rarely the case. Invest into things that can't be destroyed, stolen, or taken away as you store up treasure not only in this life, but the life to come.

A wise man is full of strength, and a man of knowledge enhances his might, for by wise guidance you can wage your war, and in abundance of counselors there is victory.

Proverbs 24:5-6 ESV

The righteous one recognizes that in order to overpower or silence her opponents, she must get godly advice. Saying 22 reveals that wise counsel can only be given to the one who humbly admits she needs help. At times, those in leadership must wage war against physical enemies, but most often our personal struggles are not with flesh and blood, but rather against the unseen forces of evil, prompting and pushing us to make unwise decisions. We may need to persuade opponents to think consistently with wisdom, yet we will more likely engage in dialogue with ourselves as we consider God's design for human behavior, seeking to align our will with his. It is foolish for anyone to do battle alone. Whom do you go to for godly advice? Make sure you get biblical counsel as you resist your enemies today, even when the enemy is your own sinful nature.

Wisdom is too high for a fool; in the gate he does not open his mouth. Whoever plans to do evil will be called a schemer. The devising of folly is sin, and the scoffer is an abomination to mankind.

Proverbs 24:7-9 ESV

According to Saying 23, when in the gate, the place where leaders of the community made decisions for the welfare of its citizens, the fool has nothing substantial to say. Lacking humility and an others-oriented focus, the fool is unable to think through Scripture and determine what would be best for society. Saying 24 reveals that the fool is not necessarily stupid as she plots and plans, but her goals are selfish. She manipulates circumstances so that she will come out on top, even at the expense of everyone around her. In time, the community becomes aware of her ploys, as she repeats the same patterns again and again. Scandal follows the schemer wherever she goes. If you are the woman who drags others down to elevate yourself, repent today. Get your heart right before the Lord. God cares very much about communities of people and will not suffer long with the one who cannot get along with the rest of the world.

If you faint in the day of adversity, your strength is small. Rescue those who are being taken away to death; hold back those who are stumbling to the slaughter. If you say, "Behold, we did not know this," does not he who weighs the heart perceive it? Does not he who keeps watch over your soul know it, and will he not repay man according to his work?

Proverbs 24:10-12 ESV

When faced with a crisis, according to Saying 25, the depth of one's character is revealed. Those who are genuinely committed to the Lord become apparent during times of hardship. When the righteous woman discovers that the guiltless are wrongly being led to death, she must exercise courage and stand up for those who have no voice. God is not pleased when justice is perverted, and as his followers, we should not sit idly when we are aware of wrongdoing. To get involved and protect the innocent, we must be willing to risk our own personal peace and safety. Realizing the potential for trouble, some will claim they weren't aware of tragedy. But God sees all, even our hearts. If we neglect to help those who are unjustly suffering, God will neglect to help us when we are in distress. Choose to stand up for the persecuted today, even if you will be inconvenienced as a result.

My son, eat honey, for it is good, and the drippings of the honeycomb are sweet to your taste. Know that wisdom is such to your soul; if you find it, there will be a future, and your hope will not be cut off.

Proverbs 24:13-14 ESV

One of the wonderful gifts the Lord graces humanity with is the ability to enjoy food. In Saying 26, the son is encouraged to experience the sweetness of honey, which was highly prized in the ancient Near East. Honey not only tastes sweet, but was also believed to have healing properties. The father then explains why the son should appreciate the gifts of God, as he makes a parallel between honey and wisdom. Just as honey is full of sweetness and healing, so too is wisdom, even more so. By embracing biblical wisdom, the son is assured of the beauty, security, and joy of heaven, that come from trusting in God and following after the Lord's design and desire for human life. Every good and perfect gift we enjoy in life comes from the Lord. As you are blessed by the pleasures of life today, realize that they are only glimpses of all that God has in the life to come for those who love him.

Lie not in wait as a wicked man against the dwelling of the righteous; do no violence to his home; for the righteous falls seven times and rises again, but the wicked stumble in times of calamity.

Proverbs 24:15-16 ESV

Though the wicked person may attempt to plunder the righteous, and even succeed temporarily, in the end God will enable the righteous to recover from the plots of the ungodly. In fact, Saying 27 reveals that God will orchestrate circumstances so that the wicked will suffer the destruction they intended for others. Ultimately, the day will transpire when we depart this life through death and face the judgment of God. The unjust will account for everything they did along with every motive behind their behavior. When their actions and attitudes are compared against God's decrees, they will be found guilty. And they will be sentenced accordingly. But the wise, who acknowledge God's authority over all of creation, humbly confess their wrongdoing and turn from their sin, placing their total trust in the person and work of Jesus, will stand in the day of judgment. The righteous truly will rise again.

Do not rejoice when your enemy falls, and let not your heart be glad when he stumbles, lest the Lord see it and be displeased, and turn away his anger from him. Fret not yourself because of evildoers, and be not envious of the wicked, for the evil man has no future; the lamp of the wicked will be put out.

Proverbs 24:17-20 ESV

According to Saying 28, God does not want his people to be cold and cruel toward others, even their enemies, but remember that every human life bears the image of God and has value to him. Although our adversaries may be arrogant, heartless, and even treat us with brutality, the Lord does not want us to add evil to evil by returning their animosity toward us with further hatred. We must stand up for what is right, but not give way to moral ugliness in the process. We have been given the free gift of God's grace and must continually seek to extend his grace to others. Saying 29 adds that God's people are not to be angry and covetous as they see the ungodly prosper. It is right to be mad when God and his character are maligned, but we are to control our fury, always hoping for the best, refraining from the desire for revenge and leaving room for the wrath of God.

My son, fear the Lord and the king, and do not join with those who do otherwise, for disaster will arise suddenly from them, and who knows the ruin that will come from them both?

Proverbs 24:21-22 ESV

According to Saying 3o, a wise life begins with a healthy fear of God and his word. The son is encouraged to fear the king, who has been entrusted with administering justice on earth. This advice would assume the king is good, but even in the presence of an unjust king, the godly person is to align her behavior with the desire of the governing authorities, as long biblical law and principles are not violated. The son is further admonished to refrain from any attempt to overthrow the leadership of the Lord and his king. To advance in status, one must come under the king's rule rather than destroy it. What authorities has God placed in your life? The wise woman yields to the desires of those over her, resisting only when her leader's will opposes the will of the Lord. If she kicks against authority, both the Lord and the king will allow negative consequences to result.

*These also are sayings of the wise.
Partiality in judging is not good.
Whoever says to the wicked, "You are
in the right," will be cursed by peoples,
abhorred by nations, but those who rebuke
the wicked will have delight, and a
good blessing will come upon them.*

Proverbs 24:23-25 ESV

Further sayings continue. When making judgments, it is wrong to show preference to the familiar or those who have potential to return the favor. The woman who declares the wicked righteous will lose credibility in her community. On the other hand, society will esteem those who stand up for truth. If you seek to walk on the path of the righteous, know that there are people who watch every move you make. When you approve of evil, they take notice. When you stand up for truth, even it if means you may lose the approval of your peers, your community recognizes that too. Whether fellow believers, the unsaved around you, or even your children, your commitment to stand up for truth impacts the way others perceive you. God and the watching world are pleased when we think and behave justly. The long-term reward for faithfulness far outweighs any short-term pleasure gained by compromise.

Whoever gives an honest answer kisses the lips. Prepare your work outside; get everything ready for yourself in the field, and after that build your house.

Proverbs 24:26-27 ESV

In the ancient Near East, when one was beneath another in social status, he bowed in deference. When one was slightly above another, the superior graciously kissed the inferior on the cheek. But when two were equal, a quick kiss on the lips was appropriate. The kiss also symbolized devotion in the Old Testament. So an honest answer is as valuable as the intimacy between two friends. God also esteems hard work. We should be able to provide for those who will live in our homes before we actually establish those homes. Our actions and our words impact the lives of those around us. We all have friends who will say what we want to hear, but rare are the ones who love us enough to tell us the truth. Be genuine today. But don't just communicate truth and callously walk away. The faithful woman speaks honestly and stands by her friends to the very end.

Be not a witness against your neighbor without cause, and do not deceive with your lips. Do not say, "I will do to him as he has done to me; I will pay the man back for what he has done."

Proverbs 24:28-29 ESV

Those who are first-hand witnesses of a crime are obligated by law to honestly testify to what they know when called to court, but the wicked person brings charges against her neighbor because of a personal grudge. This woman twists or embellishes the facts to make her neighbor appear guilty, hoping to get revenge for any wrong she feels she has incurred at the hand of her opponent. Although God's law provides for justice through the legal system, the Lord does not approve of personal retaliation among his people. In fact, the recipients of God's mercy and grace are called to extend the same mercy and grace to others, even their enemies. The one who truly trusts in the Lord would rather be wronged than disrupt the welfare of the community and bring shame to the cause of Christ by demanding payback for any injustice (often trivial) she believes she has suffered.

I passed by the field of a sluggard, by the vineyard of a man lacking sense, and behold, it was all overgrown with thorns; the ground was covered with nettles, and its stone wall was broken down.

Proverbs 24:30-31 ESV

The father described an occasion in which he observed the vineyard of a lazy man. The vineyard had the potential to bring forth prized fruit, and yet it required patience, care, and diligence to maintain its productivity. This particular vineyard no longer produced anything edible. Its walls lay in shambles and it was overrun with weeds. It became worthless, standing as a testimony to its owner's foolish behavior. Like the sluggard, we can grow lazy and tired of hard work. But letting fields become dilapidated is never worth it. Maybe you don't own a vineyard, but you have been entrusted with much, including your relationships. Are you putting in the required energy and effort to maintain intimacy in your marriage, healthy friendships, and continual dependence upon the Lord? If not, determine to get to work. God can bring life even to the barren places when we are willing to do things his way.

Then I saw and considered it; I looked and received instruction. A little sleep, a little slumber, a little folding of the hands to rest, and poverty will come upon you like a robber, and want like an armed man.

Proverbs 24:32-34 ESV

The father revealed to his son the wisdom he gleaned from observing the sluggard's vineyard. He learned that the one who turns from work and diligence for more sleep, or for folding the hands in rest rather than using them for labor, will end up impoverished. The lazy man rested while others planted and tended their fields, and when harvest time came, the sluggard had no produce. With no produce, he had nothing to sell to generate income, and financial lack pounced upon him like an unexpected thief or an advancing soldier. His opportunity passed, and the prospect of financial blessing was gone. It is foolish to reject hard work. The one who continually seeks a path of ease will end up without much to show for her time on this planet. Whether it is physical or spiritual work, don't neglect to do good while you have the occasion. You never know when your window of opportunity will come to an end.

These also are proverbs of Solomon which the men of Hezekiah king of Judah copied. It is the glory of God to conceal things, but the glory of kings is to search things out. As the heavens for height, and the earth for depth, so the heart of kings is unsearchable.

Proverbs 25:1-3 ESV

Hezekiah's copyists transposed the sayings of Solomon from extant scrolls to new documents, often arranging the material by subject. As a king is above his people, so God is above the king. There are things the king will never know about God, and things the citizens of a realm will never know about the king. However, those whom God establishes as leaders do their job rightly by investigating matters, working hard to discover truth. Those who rule need not reveal everything they unearth to their subjects, but a good leader is diligent to observe the affairs of her people, engaging with and thinking through the dilemmas of those in her realm. Whom are you in leadership over? Do you research the controversies brewing and assessments made? Though it requires self-sacrifice and even the risk of misunderstanding, the good leader manages those underneath her with patience, thoughtfulness, and care.

Take away the dross from the silver, and the smith has material for a vessel; take away the wicked from the presence of the king, and his throne will be established in righteousness.

Proverbs 25:4-5 ESV

The metal worker must remove impurities from his silver before he can create pieces. In the same way, wicked officials must be extracted from the king's court for the ruler to lead with success. When those who are sinful and self-seeking are taken out of leadership, the realm thrives under just rule. When the ungodly are permitted to remain as advisors, their wicked thoughts infect and influence the decision-making of even the righteous rulers around them and the entire community suffers as a result. In the same way, when making decisions, it is wise to seek out the counsel of godly people. Choose to get input regarding your choices, but be sure the input you receive is from godly sources. Although it may be difficult, negative and divisive people must be removed from our inner circle. Lasting victory comes when leadership teams are focused on the welfare of their community rather than personal success.

Do not put yourself forward in the king's presence or stand in the place of the great, for it is better to be told, "Come up here," than to be put lower in the presence of a noble.

Proverbs 25:6-7 ESV

It is unwise for those under the king's authority to force entry into his inner circle or attempt to reason with the members of his council. The one who pushes to the top often views her ideas and contributions as having more value than they actually do. Instead, the woman who seeks a position of increased influence should wait for her superiors to ask her to join in on their discussions, or she risks being asked to leave. When she's asked to step down, she faces personal humiliation as it becomes evident to all that she isn't as sharp as she believes herself to be. The prudent woman will faithfully and patiently wait for promotion rather than shoving to the front of the line. Well-informed, forward-thinking, and faithful servants will be promoted when the time is right. Make sure you keep an accurate view of your abilities, while loyally performing the role you've been entrusted with today.

What your eyes have seen do not hastily bring into court, for what will you do in the end, when your neighbor puts you to shame? Argue your case with your neighbor himself, and do not reveal another's secret, lest he who hears you bring shame upon you, and your ill repute have no end.

Proverbs 25:8-10 ESV

Although one may have witnessed what she believes to be a wrongdoing, she may have only part of the puzzle and falsely accuse the innocent. The witness will look foolish when it becomes evident that she failed to get the entire story, and instead jumped to conclusions rooted in her negative opinion of others. Furthermore, if it turns out that she made the charges because of a personal dispute, it will become obvious that the accuser should have sought to make peace with her neighbor on her own without involving others, preventing disgrace in the community. Do you "have the dirt" on someone else in your family, circle of friends, or church? The godly woman will refrain from letting others know while working to reconcile with her neighbor herself. In the end, the community remembers the unjust way the event was handled rather than the charges themselves. Work things out privately, sparing the watching world from your personal drama.

A word fitly spoken is like apples of gold in a setting of silver. Like a gold ring or an ornament of gold is a wise reprover to a listening ear.

Proverbs 25:11-12 ESV

The fitly spoken word results in a wise decision. The round apple, along with its fragrant smell, illustrates the beauty of a good choice that often results from the careful gathering of information. The silver setting complements the aroma of the apple like wise words in a proper setting. Both the one who speaks good words, the wise reprover, and the one who embraces the wisdom, the listening ear, are valuable. Do you invest in others by gently speaking truth to them at the proper time? Do you encourage them when they are suffering, helping them to join you on the path of righteousness? Or does it feel like too much work for you to pour into those who are broken? As long as a person is willing to hear, keep speaking God's truth to her soul. Honest words, spoken with gentleness and respect, often generate permanent and positive change in the lives of those who receive their instruction.

Like the cold of snow in the time of harvest is a faithful messenger to those who send him; he refreshes the soul of his masters. Like clouds and wind without rain is a man who boasts of a gift he does not give.

Proverbs 25:13-14 ESV

Harvest time occurred during the hottest months of the year, and to energize the laborers, people were sent to the high mountains to obtain snow, which was used to cool beverages and refresh weary workers. In the same way, the one who brings an honest report to her boss is like an invigorating drink. Even if the news isn't positive, at least it is true. The message recipient can go on to make wise decisions, rooted in faithfully transmitted information. Clouds potentially meant rain, and much-needed showers for crops and the sustenance of life. The person who promises to give and yet doesn't follow through is as disappointing and discouraging as clouds without water. The dishonest woman is cruel and heartless. What about you? Do live up to the promises you make? It's better to think before you speak than to get someone's hopes up and not follow through.

With patience a ruler may be persuaded, and a soft tongue will break a bone. If you have found honey, eat only enough for you, lest you have your fill of it and vomit it. Let your foot be seldom in your neighbor's house, lest he have his fill of you and hate you.

Proverbs 25:15-17 ESV

The gentle person brings wisdom to others, helping them to see things from God's perspective rather than their own. In contrast to hard bones which frame the body, the soft tongue or carefully chosen words are able to shatter the most resistant opponent. Honey is sweet and beneficial, but like all good things, must be enjoyed in moderation. In the same way, we must employ reasonableness in relationships. Though friendship is a blessing, we all need personal space. Don't overstay your welcome. When you want to get your point across, do you raise your voice? Or do you remain composed, yet state things in a mean and hurtful way? Neither method is as effective as speaking the truth with gentleness and respect. Don't interfere with God's work by jumping between the Lord and the person you are advising. Move out of the way, giving others opportunity to hear from the Spirit, rather than just you.

A man who bears false witness against his neighbor is like a war club, or a sword, or a sharp arrow. Trusting in a treacherous man in time of trouble is like a bad tooth or a foot that slips. Whoever sings songs to a heavy heart is like one who takes off a garment on a cold day, and like vinegar on soda.

Proverbs 25:18-20 ESV

The ancient warrior used special weapons for different types of battle. The war club was effective for fighting up close. The sword was also for close up fighting, yet it kept some space between opponents; for battling at a distance, the fighter chose the arrow to defeat his enemies. A neighbor who turns against her friend is as lethal as any of these weapons. The associate who is not reliable is like a rotten tooth or feet that fail to hold up the body. Both are a huge disappointment to the one who trusts in their support. Finally, the friend who sings joyful songs to the discouraged is like taking a warm jacket off in the cold air, pouring stinging vinegar on a wound, or mixing two substances that create a violent explosion. Be sensitive to your friends' needs. When they are broken, grieve with them. When they rejoice, then you can laugh and celebrate.

If your enemy is hungry, give him bread to eat, and if he is thirsty, give him water to drink, for you will heap burning coals on his head, and the Lord will reward you.

Proverbs 25:21-22 ESV

The wise father teaches his son that when he sees the neighbor who hates him in need, hungry, or thirsty, he should give his enemy food to quench his appetite or water to quench his thirst. Why in the world should the son respond with kindness to one who hates him? By doing this, the son will drive his enemy to repentance, and in addition, God will repay the kindness. The burning coals mentioned are probably the good deeds themselves, which create a sense of shame within the hateful neighbor. The reward God promises may even refer to reconciliation between the two who are at odds. How do you treat those who set themselves against you? Do you extend kindness to them in the same way Jesus extends his kindness to you? Or do you demand repayment from those who have hurt your feelings? God's children should be known as compassionate and not vengeful.

*The north wind brings forth rain,
and a backbiting tongue, angry looks.
It is better to live in a corner of the
housetop than in a house shared with
a quarrelsome wife.*

Proverbs 25:23-24 ESV

Just as the north wind brings cold temperatures and a sharp chill to the air, the gossip or the slanderer's words generate icy stares from the community toward the one whose reputation she's trashed. The damage is done secretly, and the victim often is clueless as to what took place. A wife's negative and hostile speech is just as ugly and injurious as the words of the slanderer. Facing the freezing wind from an unprotected rooftop is preferable to living with a bickering spouse. So much harm can result from our sinful use of words. We may think we are powerful or clever because we can gossip or nag or manipulate others and end up getting what we want, but in the end God knows exactly what's going on. If you are someone who pushes and pushes until you get your way, today is the day to stop. Put your trust in God rather than your incessant words.

Like cold water to a thirsty soul, so is good news from a far country. Like a muddied spring or a polluted fountain is a righteous man who gives way before the wicked. It is not good to eat much honey, nor is it glorious to seek one's own glory.

Proverbs 25:25-27 ESV

Cold water refreshed the exhausted and overworked body. The anxious soul could also grow exhausted awaiting good news about a loved one far away. The report may have taken weeks or months to receive. In both cases, the righteous one was called to patiently wait and endure hardship. The upright woman who caves in to temptation, joining the wicked, is as much of a let-down as contaminated water. The water, which had the potential to bring refreshment and life, became polluted and ended up good for nothing. To exalt self is as foolish as eating too much honey. Both led to unwanted problems. What temptation are you facing today? You may think you can handle a little compromise and flirt with unrighteousness, but in the end there's far more at stake than just you. When you stumble, so do those who are watching.

A man without self-control is like a city broken into and left without walls. Like snow in summer or rain in harvest, so honor is not fitting for a fool. Like a sparrow in its flitting, like a swallow in its flying, a curse that is causeless does not alight.

Proverbs 25:28-26:2 ESV

A plundered city, left without walls, has no way to defend its citizens. Strangely, the woman without self-control is like the helpless city. Her failure to keep her emotions subdued leads to her ruin. Her passions drive her thoughts and actions rather than the wisdom of the Lord. She makes foolish decisions, and must live with the consequences of impatient and impulsive behavior. She is a liability to her community and easy prey for the enemy. She's eagerly lured into sin and quickly chases after temptation. When a community elevates this type of person, things are upside down and as out of place as summer snow or rain at harvest time. To curse the righteous is as ineffective as trying to ground a bird in flight. How well do you control your emotions? If you are tossed around by your feelings, call out to God for help. Seek his face, trust his word, and rely on his Spirit today.

A whip for the horse, a bridle for the donkey, and a rod for the back of fools. Answer not a fool according to his folly, lest you be like him yourself. Answer a fool according to his folly, lest he be wise in his own eyes.

Proverbs 26:3-5 ESV

The charioteer used a whip to drive his horses ahead. A bridle was used to direct the path of the donkey, even along difficult and unstable grounds. In the same way, the rod, or force, is necessary to drive and direct the fool, who refuses the way of wisdom. Because of the fool's lack of understanding, the righteous woman must be thoughtful and even shrewd when communicating with the unwise. The upright should never reply to the fool's insults with further insults. In doing so, she would become foolish like him. At the same time, when the fool boasts as if his own logic is superior to the wisdom from God, it's time for the righteous to speak up and show the fool the error of his reasoning. We must never behave like the fool, yet we must respond intelligently to his stupidity. In both cases, the hope is that the fool will wise up and ultimately repent.

Whoever sends a message by the hand of a fool cuts off his own feet and drinks violence. Like a lame man's legs, which hang useless, is a proverb in the mouth of fools.

Proverbs 26:6-7 ESV

When recruiting help, turn to those who have proven trustworthy. If you discover a reliable and like-minded person to labor with, it's as if your two hands have become four, and your feet have also doubled in number. Twice the amount of good work can be accomplished. But entrusting a fool with your message is as dumb as cutting off your own feet or drinking poison. The lame man may have legs and the potential to walk, but yet because of impairment, his legs are completely useless to him. In the same way, a foolish man can utter a wise statement, but because he doesn't put wisdom into practice, it is equally useless. It makes no impact on his behavior and can actually generate a false sense of security. Even if you are desperate for help today, don't turn to the fool. Wait for someone who is humble and teachable rather than one who rejects God's wisdom.

Like one who binds the stone in the sling is one who gives honor to a fool. Like a thorn that goes up into the hand of a drunkard is a proverb in the mouth of fools. Like an archer who wounds everyone is one who hires a passing fool or drunkard.

Proverbs 26:8-10 ESV

The sling was made from a long strip of leather with a wide middle to hold a stone. When properly thrown, the stone traveled long distances and became a very effective offense or defense. This weapon would be useless if the rock was attached or bound to the sling. As absurd as binding a stone in a sling is giving honor to a fool. Gracing the fool with authority could damage the entire community. An intoxicated person may wave a thorn bush around, looking for a fight, and in the same way, words of wisdom, taken out of context and misused by the fool, are spiritually dangerous. The fool is also incompetent when it comes to work. The one who puts confidence in a fool or a drunk is as unwise as someone who haphazardly shoots arrows without taking aim. A lot of people may end up hurt as a result. Resist any desire to place your hope in a foolish person.

Like a dog that returns to his vomit is a fool who repeats his folly. Do you see a man who is wise in his own eyes? There is more hope for a fool than for him.

Proverbs 26:11-12 ESV

Although dogs were domesticated in the ancient Near East, they were generally considered unclean animals because of their often repulsive practices. Those who have owned a dog know how disgusting it is to watch their pet choke up its own food and spit it out, only to re-consume it. The process is gross. Equally nauseating is the fool who doesn't learn from her mistakes. From heaven's perspective, when she repeats her sinful behavior over and over, she acts like the dog. But there is still hope for the fool. In fact, it's better to be one who returns to her vomit than to be unteachable. The fool still retains some potential to learn from her mistakes. What about you? Are there sinful habits you keep returning to again and again? If so, ask the Lord to help you gain victory over your ungodly desires. Pray that God would reveal to your soul what things look like from his perspective.

The sluggard says, "There is a lion in the road! There is a lion in the streets!" As a door turns on its hinges, so does a sluggard on his bed.

Proverbs 26:13-14 ESV

Can you imagine someone saying she couldn't get out of bed to go to work because a lion crouched in the driveway or the nearest intersection? The idle person is an expert in fabricating ridiculous claims to justify her laziness. She's able to continually come up with excuses for not doing as she should, postponing her obligations until a supposedly more favorable time. A door swings back and forth without making any actual progress because it's attached to its hinges, and so the sluggard turns back and forth on her bed, never making progress because she's attached to the comforts of home. Laziness results in wasted life. We can believe we work hard and could never be accused of laziness, yet we may continually procrastinate when it comes to spiritual disciplines, such as Bible reading or prayer. Do you think the Lord sees you as a spiritual sluggard? If so, get off the couch today.

The sluggard buries his hand in the dish; it wears him out to bring it back to his mouth. The sluggard is wiser in his own eyes than seven men who can answer sensibly.

Proverbs 26:15-16 ESV

Although the sluggard has access to food, it's too much for her to bring it up to her mouth, so she doesn't eat. The thought of working just wears her out. She sits and does nothing, becoming totally deluded. She believes she has more sense than seven advisors with a proven and wise track record. You may think this doesn't apply to you at all, but don't be quick to dismiss the insight here. Are there areas of your life where the Scripture exhorts you to a certain behavior, the Spirit convicts your heart, your godly friends give you similar advice, and yet you don't do or not do what you are called to? Maybe you are the spiritual sluggard who thinks she's going to come to God on her own terms rather than his. What about your spiritual disciplines? Do you know you should pray, but it's too hard? Listen to wisdom and turn from spiritual laziness today.

Whoever meddles in a quarrel not his own is like one who takes a passing dog by the ears. Like a madman who throws firebrands, arrows, and death is the man who deceives his neighbor and says, "I am only joking!"

Proverbs 26:17-19 ESV

Every community has its resident busybody. She's the woman who just can't seem to mind her own business, but instead meddles in the affairs of others. The busybody is as foolish as the person who grabs a wild dog by its sensitive ears, risking serious injury. Another stupid person is the one who enjoys watching others experience harm, only to brush it off as a joke. The insensitive person fails to distinguish between what is funny and what is foolish. Although she appears surprised at the suffering that results from her prank, she knew the risk involved. Her problem stems from her lack of compassion for others. If a dispute doesn't involve you, stay out of it. Mind your own business. There are many productive things you could be doing with your time. Choose to focus today on things that build up rather than tear down.

For lack of wood the fire goes out, and where there is no whisperer, quarreling ceases. As charcoal to hot embers and wood to fire, so is a quarrelsome man for kindling strife. The words of a whisperer are like delicious morsels; they go down into the inner parts of the body.

Proverbs 26:20-22 ESV

When a fire runs out of wood, the flames die. In the same way, when the slanderer stops fueling a fight, the commotion ends. On the other hand, when the slanderer is acting in full force, contention is rampant. In order for a community to be at peace, the one who stirs up strife must be removed. Just as yeast spreads throughout dough, so do the manipulative words of the troublemaker. In time, the entire neighborhood feels the effects of her disruptive behavior. Those who listen to or ingest the whispered information the gossip communicates are likewise guilty of participating in harmful talk. Although it's tempting to join in when the whisperer lowers her voice to enlighten you about another, you must resist the lure. Her material is loaded with half-truths, exaggerations, and spins she puts on information in an attempt to cast herself in a favorable light. Walk away from gossip today, removing yourself from inaccurate reports about others.

Like the glaze covering an earthen vessel are fervent lips with an evil heart. Whoever hates disguises himself with his lips and harbors deceit in his heart; when he speaks graciously, believe him not, for there are seven abominations in his heart;

Proverbs 26:23-25 ESV

Metallic glazes were used on ceramics to make them appear shiny and more expensive than they actually were. Flattering words operate in the same way, providing an insincere gloss that misleads the naïve. The one who uses flattery to manipulate is driven by selfish motives, hoping to gain something from her deceptive speech. A hateful heart can be cloaked in words of praise, providing a cover for the true intentions. We often recognize the mean spirit behind hurtful words, but we can be so duped by praise from others. How do you respond to flattery? Do you think logically, realizing that you really aren't the most beautiful or talented or upright person in the world? Or do you fall for the flatterer's scheme, showing unnatural favor to those who speak well of you? Sometimes what we want to hear doesn't line up with the truth. Listen to those who love you enough to be honest.

though his hatred be covered with deception, his wickedness will be exposed in the assembly. Whoever digs a pit will fall into it, and a stone will come back on him who starts it rolling. A lying tongue hates its victims, and a flattering mouth works ruin.

Proverbs 26:26-28 ESV

Some are so wretched that they seek to destroy people and communities from the inside out. They despise those who live according to God's standards and want to bring chaos among the people of the Lord. These miserable people are unhappy and feel better when they pull others down into the mud with them. They use flattery and manipulation to gain entrance into the confidences of those around them, and when the time is just right, they go in for the kill. But any apparent victory is only for a season. God sees and will allow the wicked woman's own iniquity to return back to her. In time, she will be discovered. Though the flatterer seeks her own good to the ruin of others, in the end she will be ruined when her manipulative and self-seeking ways become exposed to the community. Beware of those who cover deceptive motives with generous words.

Do not boast about tomorrow, for you do not know what a day may bring. Let another praise you, and not your own mouth; a stranger, and not your own lips.

Proverbs 27:1-2 ESV

It is pleasant to others and pleasing to the Lord when we are humble. We often agree that we don't know what the future holds, but we can forget that the future is as near as the next time the sun rises. None of us knows what will happen tomorrow. God alone is omniscient, or all knowing, and he doesn't share that attribute with any created being. It is wise to make plans for the future, but we must always keep in mind that God is the one who allows those plans to prosper. God also retains the right to thwart our agendas whenever he sees fit. Those who praise themselves are at odds with the Lord and with their community. No one enjoys the company of a prideful and arrogant person. In fact, the real friend is the one who brings praise and encouragement to those she loves. Be a good friend today by drawing attention to others rather than yourself.

A stone is heavy, and sand is weighty, but a fool's provocation is heavier than both. Wrath is cruel, anger is overwhelming, but who can stand before jealousy?

Proverbs 27:3-4 ESV

The stone and sand weigh much, putting stress and strain on the one who chooses to carry them. The stone refers to an incredibly heavy rock, and the sand describes all the sand of the world's beaches. The heaviness of these things is so immense that their burden is impossible to bear. Yet, the enticement of the fool is even more unbearable than these great weights. The fool will relentlessly wear down the righteous, as long as the upright allows his ridiculous influence. Anger and wrath are crushing as they vent their fury. But even more merciless is jealousy, which includes anger and wrath, but is driven by passion. The one who arouses jealousy in another is stupid. Have you ever been provoked by a foolish person? Maybe you've behaved in a way you later regretted because you were pushed to your limits. Be wise today, and keep your distance from fools. If you don't, you'll end up just like them.

*Better is open rebuke than hidden love.
Faithful are the wounds of a friend;
profuse are the kisses of an enemy.*

Proverbs 27:5-6 ESV

We usually don't enjoy correcting our friends and loved ones. At times, it can seem easier to let their wrong behavior go unaddressed to avoid conflict and strife. But real love considers the well being of others and so is willing to risk the awkwardness associated with bringing truth. It is better to honestly rebuke sinful practices than cower behind the desire to be liked. The truth can feel painful, even like wounds, but a real friend is willing to create discomfort in a relationship if it means the other party might embrace godly thinking and behavior. The one who only tells us what we want to hear is as destructive to our soul as an enemy. If we are really going to love our neighbor the same way we love ourselves, we must be honest. Regardless of the outcome, we must be ready and willing to humbly dispense truth to others.

One who is full loathes honey, but to one who is hungry everything bitter is sweet. Like a bird that strays from its nest is a man who strays from his home.

Proverbs 27:7-8 ESV

The person whose belly is full has no room left for dessert. In the same way, the man who is sexually satisfied in his marriage is less likely to be lured by opportunities for infidelity. To the one who is famished, even bitter food is better than nothing, and so the sexually starved husband is more easily won over by the adulteress. The wife who withholds sex from her husband may push him to leave her in the same way troubling circumstances drive a bird from its nest. When he leaves and roams the town, his likelihood of unfaithfulness is increased. Although it may be difficult at times, the wise man is called to remain at home and be faithful to his wife. God has called the husband and wife to the most intimate of all earthly relationships. If married, actively pursue a spiritual, emotional, and physical relationship with your husband today (or tonight).

Oil and perfume make the heart glad, and the sweetness of a friend comes from his earnest counsel. Do not forsake your friend and your father's friend, and do not go to your brother's house in the day of your calamity. Better is a neighbor who is near than a brother who is far away. Be wise, my son, and make my heart glad, that I may answer him who reproaches me.

Proverbs 27:9-11 ESV

Olive oil brings relief to dry skin, incense creates a pleasant fragrance, and the committed friend is a great source of joy. During a time of crisis, it's better to turn to a close friend nearby and accessible than a blood relative who is distant and far off. One of life's highest blessings is true friendship with one who is steadfast and available through good and bad times. The father entrusts his son with the responsibility to be like-minded with him, prepared to defend his honor and his name against any adversary. It is important that family and friends stick together, ready and willing to weather the storms of life as a team. Would your friends say you are a source of joy in their lives? Do you take time to listen, rejoicing in their victories and grieving with their heartaches? Choose to get your eyes off yourself and be a good friend to someone else today.

The prudent sees danger and hides himself, but the simple go on and suffer for it. Take a man's garment when he has put up security for a stranger, and hold it in pledge when he puts up security for an adulteress. Whoever blesses his neighbor with a loud voice, rising early in the morning, will be counted as cursing.

Proverbs 27:12-14 ESV

The one who is wise thinks about the potential of financial bondage. When an opportunity to enter into a financial contract arises, this person carefully considers the long-term problems associated with any monetary arrangement, and walks away from unwise transactions. The fool signs on the dotted line, thinking she can agree now and deal with it later. Some carelessly agree to put up money for the man who is borrowing to pay the adulteress. Then both parties are enslaved. The wise son will flee from both the lender and the debtor. The neighbor who makes a fuss over blessing and praising another neighbor, even drawing much attention to his exaggerated words, boasting early and loudly, will become a curse. Others may miss the hypocrisy of her actions, but not the Lord. By drawing attention to her neighbor, she truly seeks to draw attention to herself. True friendship is manifested in actions rather than words.

A continual dripping on a rainy day and a quarrelsome wife are alike; to restrain her is to restrain the wind or to grasp oil in one's right hand.

Proverbs 27:15-16 ESV

A nonstop leak in rainy weather and a wife who pushes for her own way are both unbearable. A man comes home hoping to find rest from the troubles of the day, but instead he is met with a defective roof and a dissatisfied wife. Both are depressing and not what he envisioned. The home should be a place of peace, but instead of retreat from the storm, the wicked wife brings thunder right into their living space. This woman should have been a source of joy to her husband, but he is left broken as he observes his circumstances in contrast to the way he imagined things to be. The quarrelsome wife thought her life would get better with marriage, but just as she was unsatisfied in her single days, she is equally unsatisfied as a wife. The woman who is disgruntled with the Lord will never be pleased in any circumstance.

November
11

Iron sharpens iron, and one man sharpens another. Whoever tends a fig tree will eat its fruit, and he who guards his master will be honored. As in water face reflects face, so the heart of man reflects the man.

Proverbs 27:18-19 ESV

A knife or sword is sharpened when it is rubbed against another piece of metal. In the same way, when two good and godly friends dialogue, they sharpen one another using words, and they are both refined as a result. It takes faithfulness to nurture a fig tree, but its fruit is sweet in the end. The one who works diligently at her job will be rewarded as well. We see our faces reflected when we look in a mirror or in a still pool of water, and we see the condition of our hearts when we look at our actions. What we do reveals who we are. A friend who is as hard as iron is a true friend. She won't bend and be dishonest when she sees compromise in your life, and she won't give up on your relationship either. Make sure you are hanging out with people who make you better rather than bring you down.

Sheol and Abaddon are never satisfied, and never satisfied are the eyes of man. The crucible is for silver, and the furnace is for gold, and a man is tested by his praise. Crush a fool in a mortar with a pestle along with crushed grain, yet his folly will not depart from him.

Proverbs 27:20-22 ESV

Death is never quenched, continually and relentlessly bringing its victims to the grave, and in the same way lustful passions are never satisfied. Unchecked, the human desire for more consumes and devours communities, families, and even individuals. True spiritual rest is found in the finished work of Christ. Just as the purity of a metal was proven through the process of heating, in the same way a person's heart is proven by whom she praises and who praises her in return. A mortar and pestle were used to grind grain, making it useful, but even crushing and pounding don't drive foolish ways from the unwise person. From a human standpoint, it may be impossible to teach the foolish, but thankfully, Jesus has the power to bring even the dead to life. Do you honor those who fear the Lord, or those who love the world? Make sure you look up to people who look up to God.

*Know well the condition of your flocks,
and give attention to your herds, for
riches do not last forever; and does a
crown endure to all generations?*

Proverbs 27:23-24 ESV

In the ancient Near East, the one who owned flocks and livestock was wealthy. He would employ servants to oversee his affairs. He would employ servants to oversee his affairs. Proper management of the wealthy man's assets required diligent effort, and the son is exhorted to remain involved in managing the estate, rather than delegating all his responsibilities to those underneath him. Animals need food, water, shelter, and care. The son must not become lazy or weary, but instead always work hard, and invest personally into his herds with kindness. He must remember the transitory nature of the things in this life, and never assume that his assets will always be there for him. The wise person recognizes that power and wealth in this life belong to her for only a brief time. Soon we will stand before the Lord, and see how the decisions we made while on earth had (or didn't have) a lasting impact. Make time for things of eternal value today.

When the grass is gone and the new growth appears and the vegetation of the mountains is gathered, the lambs will provide your clothing, and the goats the price of a field. There will be enough goats' milk for your food, for the food of your household and maintenance for your girls.

Proverbs 27:25-27 ESV

The wise man keeps an eye on the affairs of his estate, working diligently to ensure his flocks are well cared for. When the grass that feeds the flocks dries up, the Lord will cause new growth to appear again. Just as God is faithful to provide for his creation, those entrusted to manage the earth must respond to his goodness with wise administration. Proper care of the flocks results in financial reward, and the upright family increases in wealth and influence. The well-tended flocks will provide for the family and even the servants, who in turn care for the flocks. Those who respond rightly to God's created order are blessed. By working within the parameters the Lord has established for his creation, harmony is established. We must not grow weary of working hard, faithfully managing the treasure and talent God has entrusted us with, while humbly acknowledging his good hand in all that we have been given.

The wicked flee when no one pursues, but the righteous are bold as a lion. When a land transgresses, it has many rulers, but with a man of understanding and knowledge, its stability will long continue. A poor man who oppresses the poor is a beating rain that leaves no food.

Proverbs 28:1-3 ESV

Those who reject the Lord live with paranoia, like people running from an enemy who isn't there. Those who love God are secure in their relationship with him and live confidently as a result. A nation of people who fear God is more stable than one who bow before none but themselves. When man is viewed as the ultimate authority, each person must watch his own back. The righteous ruler must lead with fairness and a fear of the Lord. Rain should stimulate prosperity and growth, and so should those who lead, but oppressive rulers are as disappointing as rains that devastate. It has been said that because the righteous fear the Lord, they don't fear people. In contrast, because the wicked don't fear God, they live in terror before men. If you are right with God today, take courage! He is in charge of every detail of your life. Boldly obey him today.

Those who forsake the law praise the wicked, but those who keep the law strive against them. Evil men do not understand justice, but those who seek the Lord understand it completely.

Proverbs 28:4-5 ESV

People who reject the Lord's wisdom, living their own way instead of submitting to God's desires, give approval to others who also turn from righteousness. Those who love the Lord resist the desire to embrace wickedness. Because the unrighteous deeds of sinners have separated them from the Lord, they aren't able to discern what is morally upright. On the other hand, those who turn to Jesus and repent of their evil behaviors are internally changed, and God places his law upon their hearts. We have all experienced peer pressure. Those we live and work among engage in activities contrary to what the Scripture teaches, and they push us to practice those behaviors with them. Though it is difficult, God's people must resist compromise. Whom you hang out with reveals what you are really like. Promote your own righteous behavior today by choosing friends who seek to be righteous as well.

Better is a poor man who walks in his integrity than a rich man who is crooked in his ways. The one who keeps the law is a son with understanding, but a companion of gluttons shames his father.

Proverbs 28:6-7 ESV

It is better to live an honest life and be destitute than to have even great wealth gained by deceitful means. The crooked man is doubly devious. First, he defrauds his neighbor to get more than he earned or deserves, and then, he passes himself off as blameless. Ironically, usually the poor man is the victim of the one both crooked and rich. Though the poor person may suffer now, the Day is coming when the Lord will make right every wrong. The wise son listens to and applies his father's teaching, but the foolish son befriends reprobates, bringing shame to his family. Unless your parents are giving you ungodly advice, it's smart to listen to them. Your mother and father probably want to see you succeed more than anyone else does. Don't be deceived into thinking they are attempting to rip you off.

Whoever multiplies his wealth by interest and profit gathers it for him who is generous to the poor. If one turns away his ear from hearing the law, even his prayer is an abomination.

Proverbs 28:8-9 ESV

Two types of people assisted the poor. The wealthy but greedy loaned money with interest, thus increasing their own wealth at the expense of the needy. The wealthy but upright supported the poor without demanding anything in return. These people gave to the poor, supporting them without demanding anything in return. With justice, God watches and manages all that transpires among men, and he orchestrates events so that the greedy end up losing, while the kind are graced with even more to give. What an honor to be the generous person whom God entrusts with his resources! When a woman refuses to listen to the Lord, the Lord refuses to listen to her. Although God hears the prayers of all people, he isn't obligated to respond to any of them. Nevertheless, he humbly chooses to answer those who have turned to him. God rejects the behavior and the cries of the wicked.

Whoever misleads the upright into an evil way will fall into his own pit, but the blameless will have a goodly inheritance. A rich man is wise in his own eyes, but a poor man who has understanding will find him out.

Proverbs 28:10-11 ESV

Because evil people desire to bring others down into darkness with them, they seek to deceive the righteous into participating in wicked behavior. Those who walk uprightly before the Lord see through the manipulation and boasting of the wealthy man steeped in pride. Although he may have little in this life, the godly poor person has insight into the schemes of the deceptive. Thus, one may lack treasure on earth but be rich in heavenly wisdom and reward. The Scripture teaches that even the godly are capable of sinning. We must guard our hearts against evil behavior by fixing our minds on God's law and seeking the help of his Spirit to strengthen us to continue in the right way. It also helps to get a couple of Christ-honoring friends to come alongside you in your battle with sinful desires. Choose to elevate God's will above your own today.

When the righteous triumph, there is great glory, but when the wicked rise, people hide themselves. Whoever conceals his transgressions will not prosper, but he who confesses and forsakes them will obtain mercy. Blessed is the one who fears the Lord always, but whoever hardens his heart will fall into calamity.

Proverbs 28:12-14 ESV

When those who rule the land are righteous, the people live openly and freely. When wicked leadership oppresses the land, the people live in fear, continually suspicious and even hiding from one another. The one who covers up her own sin will not be successful, but the one who confesses her wrongdoing to God will find the favor of the Lord. Instead of trying to bury your sin to hide your transgressions from the all-seeing and all-knowing God, admit your guilt. Then ask God to help you finish the process of confession by turning from your wicked ways and choosing to live consistently with his design. The one who fears the Lord, trembling at the thought of displeasing him, will be blessed, while the defiant and stubborn person will fall in defeat. If you want to be happy tomorrow, then be afraid of offending God today.

Like a roaring lion or a charging bear is a wicked ruler over a poor people. A ruler who lacks understanding is a cruel oppressor, but he who hates unjust gain will prolong his days.

Proverbs 28:15-16 ESV

An evil ruler uses his position of authority for selfish and unjust personal gain. A roaring lion is ferocious, and when hungry, it will do whatever necessary to satisfy its desires. A charging bear aggressively attacks without warning, overwhelming its victims. The wicked leader is as terrifying as these two beasts, plundering the poor without compassion. The unwise ruler foolishly exploits his power, preying upon those who look to him for protection and provision. But the honest and upright leader makes choices for the good of the community. His deeds will endure, even into the life to come. Just as rulers leave a legacy, either of terror or compassion, so do we. If those you have authority over were to summarize your leadership today, would they characterize you as faithful and kind, or harsh and exacting? How will you be remembered in ten, or even a hundred years from now?

If one is burdened with the blood of another, he will be a fugitive until death; let no one help him. Whoever walks in integrity will be delivered, but he who is crooked in his ways will suddenly fall.

Proverbs 28:17-18 ESV

God created humans in his image and graced each one with a conscience. Though we can harden our hearts to the sense of fairness God has placed within us, most are sensitive toward the internal accusations which arise when we sin, bearing witness to our violation of God's law. The one who has taken the life of an innocent man is tormented. The deceptive person will land in a pit. But God will help those who are devoted to him, following his ways and trusting in his goodness. God gifts us with consciences to convict us, so that we might repent. There will be times when those we love undergo spiritual struggles as the Holy Spirit exposes their guilt, leaving them broken before the Lord. Although tempting, it's not always right to rescue them from their spiritual pain, and possibly get in the way of the Lord. God's comfort is for those who turn from sin to Jesus.

Whoever works his land will have plenty of bread, but he who follows worthless pursuits will have plenty of poverty. A faithful man will abound with blessings, but whoever hastens to be rich will not go unpunished. To show partiality is not good, but for a piece of bread a man will do wrong.

Proverbs 28:19-21 ESV

The person who earns a living through honest and faithful labor will have all she needs, while the one who chases after "get rich quick" schemes and manipulative ways to defraud others of their money ends up with nothing. God will punish the woman who schemes to grab a quick dollar, often by capitalizing upon the kindness of others. Some gain resources by showing partiality or ruling favorably on another's behalf when bribed, even perverting justice for as little as one meal. We will continually face offers of fast money and ways to strike it rich without hard work. These proposals usually attempt to capitalize our desire to spend more time with our families and less at work. But God honors the traditional way of making money. Compromise for financial gain never pays off in the end. Walk away from schemes that require little and promise big.

A stingy man hastens after wealth and does not know that poverty will come upon him. Whoever rebukes a man will afterward find more favor than he who flatters with his tongue. Whoever robs his father or his mother and says, "That is no transgression," is a companion to a man who destroys.

Proverbs 28:22-24 ESV

The greedy person seeks wealth by exploiting others, and yet her thirst for financial gain will never be satisfied. She leaves this planet with nothing but regret regarding the selfish choices she embraced. God values a sincere woman. The one who tells the truth may not be initially applauded like the flatterer, but in the end, her honesty will be esteemed and rewarded. It's tragic when a woman is so desperate for financial gain that she swindles her own parents out of their wealth. She may rationalize her wicked behavior, thinking that whatever her parents own is actually hers, but to wrongfully take what belongs to her mother and father is abhorrent. The ungodly person believes her parents owe her something, blaming them for her own failures, or expecting them to provide financially. Think of a way to bless your parents today by giving to rather than taking from their resources.

A greedy man stirs up strife, but the one who trusts in the Lord will be enriched. Whoever trusts in his own mind is a fool, but he who walks in wisdom will be delivered. Whoever gives to the poor will not want, but he who hides his eyes will get many a curse. When the wicked rise, people hide themselves, but when they perish, the righteous increase.

Proverbs 28:25-28 ESV

The one who trusts in the Lord, working hard while remaining content, will be blessed. This is the woman who follows after the wisdom of the Lord, obeying him and trusting in his word. The woman who is determined to live for herself, doing what she feels and ignoring the counsel of the Lord, will finish the book of her life with pages steeped in regret. Our confidence in God is revealed by the way we deal with the resources he has entrusted to us. Are we stingy, hoarding what we have and clamoring for more, or do we open our hands to others and share what God has graced us with? God supports the kind and compassionate woman. When wickedness reigns, people hide, but when the righteous prevail, goodness and mercy flourish and God is exalted. The greedy woman is never satisfied. She misses the joy in what she has because she's always grumbling about what she wants.

He who is often reproved, yet stiffens his neck, will suddenly be broken beyond healing. When the righteous increase, the people rejoice, but when the wicked rule, the people groan.

Proverbs 29:1-2 ESV

Listening to wisdom is necessary for life. The one who rejects the wise counsel offered to her by the Proverbs and the Scripture will be cut off. The term "stiff necked" occurs throughout the Old Testament, describing an animal that is stubborn, unsubmissive, defiant, and rejects the yoke placed upon its neck in order to work the land. In the same way, a person who stiffens her neck refuses to heed advice. Corrupt leadership creates misery within communities, and when leaders are self-seeking, the people are broken. But when good and kind rulers rise to power, there is joy and hope in the land. There will come a time for all who are hardhearted when the chance to repent is no longer available. The fool who refuses the Lord's instruction and is determined to do things her way will eventually reach the point of hopelessness. Why not soften your neck and fully submit yourself to God's desires today?

He who loves wisdom makes his father glad, but a companion of prostitutes squanders his wealth. By justice a king builds up the land, but he who exacts gifts tears it down.

Proverbs 29:3-4 ESV

The wise son loves truth, and by putting into practice the wisdom he's gained, keeps himself far from the wicked. The obedient son's father is full of joy, grateful that the son listened to his instruction and thankful that the son will have a blessed life, free from the baggage and scars which accompany sinful choices. The parents trust the godly son with no fear of how he will manage the family resources. As a son can ruin his family through foolish choices, so can a king destroy a nation by his wicked decisions. The king should be trusted to advocate for the weaker members of the community. The ruler who receives bribes, willing to pervert justice for financial gain, destroys the nation. When the land is attacked, the broken people have little desire to defend their unjust leaders and the community falls. If you are feeling weary today, don't give up. Wisdom will never let you down.

A man who flatters his neighbor spreads a net for his feet. An evil man is ensnared in his transgression, but a righteous man sings and rejoices.

Proverbs 29:5-6 ESV

The hunter carefully lays a net to trap his prey, and in the same way, the flatterer selects choice words to seduce his victim. Eventually, the one who manipulates words for personal gain will be ensnared by her own strategies. The wise woman cautiously observes the words and actions of others, walking freely without fear as a result. She isn't won over by inflated praises. Many wise people have been toppled not only by hurtful words, but by smooth talk as well. How do you respond to overly gracious words about your character, your abilities, or your appearance? Do you become puffed up and primed for the kill? Or do you accept compliments tactfully and with an attitude of reasonableness? The one who builds you up may be the first to rip you down. Watch out for agenda-driven flattery, resisting the desire to think more highly of yourself than you ought.

A righteous man knows the rights of the poor; a wicked man does not understand such knowledge. Scoffers set a city aflame, but the wise turn away wrath. If a wise man has an argument with a fool, the fool only rages and laughs, and there is no quiet.

Proverbs 29:7-9 ESV

The evil person is so self focused that she doesn't think about how her behavior impacts others around her, especially those who have less. But the one who is upright considers how her actions may exploit the disadvantaged, showing compassion to all. Mockers ignore the needs of others, joyfully destroying if it means getting their own way. Those who are wise work to protect the well-being and integrity of the community, rejecting the perversion of fairness. When at odds, the wise person calmly defers to the judicial system for protection, but the fool laughs and scoffs at the claims up the upright. The righteous reject the fool's babble, avoiding strife. When allured, refuse to allow your emotions to override logic. Stick to what makes sense, trusting the Lord for vindication. Though a fool may entice you to engage in his nonsense, even repeatedly, stand firm and resist temptation today.

Bloodthirsty men hate one who is blameless and seek the life of the upright. A fool gives full vent to his spirit, but a wise man quietly holds it back.

Proverbs 29:10-11 ESV

Wicked fools can't stand the honesty of godly men and women. Determined to prohibit the righteous from interfering with their schemes, the hatred of some is quelled only when the upright are eliminated, even murdered. The fool openly vents his anger. When he is mad, all will know it. The wise woman remains composed when provoked, refraining from ranting and retaliating. She trusts in the goodness and the sovereignty of the Lord, and her inner spirit remains at peace. Even though circumstances may rage around her like the tumultuous sea, she is calm and even-keeled, confident that God allows only what's best for her soul. She keeps her feelings in check, continually considering how her reaction to the day's events will impact those around her. Are your emotions controlling you? If so, ask the Lord to help you to calm down, keeping your heart and mind focused on the things he values.

December

1

> If a ruler listens to falsehood, all his officials will be wicked. The poor man and the oppressor meet together; the Lord gives light to the eyes of both. If a king faithfully judges the poor, his throne will be established forever.

Proverbs 29:12-14 ESV

The leader who listens to lies, making unjust decisions while oppressing the poor and unfortunate, will infect those underneath him with the same sinful mentality. In an attempt to impress the evil ruler, his subjects imitate his actions, and eventually the entire kingdom erodes. The poor, along with his persecutor, depend upon the Lord for the ability to see and experience the created world. Regardless of extreme difference in rank within the social structure, they both bear the image of God, and in that sense are more alike than different. The oppressor should respect the dignity of poor man, and the poor man should not despise the strength and riches of his oppressor. The leader who doesn't bend his ear toward the wicked, but faithfully acknowledges the poor, will be blessed by the Lord. Whom are you at odds with today? Ask God to grace you with the ability to see your enemy through the lens of compassion today.

The rod and reproof give wisdom, but a child left to himself brings shame to his mother. When the wicked increase, transgression increases, but the righteous will look upon their downfall. Discipline your son, and he will give you rest; he will give delight to your heart.

Proverbs 29:15-17 ESV

Parents are called to discipline their children, and parents who refuse to punish their disobedient kids will suffer for their negligence later. Though it can be exhausting, we must continue to chastise our children's immoral behavior. Although the behavior of the wicked may succeed for a moment, it will not prosper in the long run. For now, the righteous must live by faith. Eventually, the godly will watch those who embraced evil suffer the wrath they deserve for their selfish and sinful actions. Rest implies a state of peace, as opposed to conflict or chaos. Parents who faithfully discipline their children will experience the delight of happy and harmonious relationships with their kids. When children are consistently corrected, the parents and the kids profit. Even if you are weary today, care about your kids enough to penalize them when they sin. God disciplines us, and we must discipline our kids as well.

December

3

Where there is no prophetic vision the people cast off restraint, but blessed is he who keeps the law. By mere words a servant is not disciplined, for though he understands, he will not respond.

Proverbs 29:18-19 ESV

When communities reject the Lord and his authority, moral law is cast aside and everyone ends up doing what is right in his own eyes. But those who know and keep the word of the Lord are happy, living consistently with God's design for human behavior. Whether a servant or a son, all who despise wisdom must suffer the consequences of their sinful actions. Mere words are often insufficient when it comes to correcting bad behavior. Penalties for transgressions tend to drive obedience more than simple conversation does. For most, traffic tickets moderate driving habits more effectively than the rules found in the handbook. Though we may resist embracing God's decrees, the wise learn that his laws are not burdensome. Just as fish thrive in water and birds soar in the air, those who keep God's law are liberated to live successfully within the parameters for which humans have been designed.

Do you see a man who is hasty in his words? There is more hope for a fool than for him. Whoever pampers his servant from childhood will in the end find him his heir. A man of wrath stirs up strife, and one given to anger causes much transgression.

Proverbs 29:20-22 ESV

Words have the power to harm others. The fool often wrongly responds in certain situations out of sheer stupidity, but the hasty woman is more calculated than the fool. This woman knows better, yet feels comfortable blurting out what's on her mind. She realizes her speech is destructive, but she doesn't care. If she's thinking it, she believes she has the right to express it to others. When servants or employees are catered to, they lose respect for the authorities over them. It is detrimental when servants or sons feel entitled and harbor ungrateful attitudes. The person who allows her anger to build up within will eventually release it in outbursts, causing harm to others. This woman enjoys being at war with others and would rather fight than forfeit. No matter what your temperament, ethnicity, or upbringing, ask God to help you manage and control your inner anger today.

December

5

One's pride will bring him low, but he who is lowly in spirit will obtain honor. The partner of a thief hates his own life; he hears the curse, but discloses nothing.

Proverbs 29:23-24 ESV

The woman who lives as if she were above those around her will be brought down, while the one who is reasonable, considering the needs of others, will be rewarded. Those who regularly seek the Lord become increasingly aware of their failures and humbly rely on God for daily strength. The proud woman is self-sufficient, having no need for the Lord's forgiveness. The one who participates with a thief has no internal peace. She is tormented by her sinful choices. The victims who have suffered at the hands of the criminals curse them and their actions, while the guilty remain silent. The woman who sins to enjoy more of life ends up losing passion for the life she sought to enhance. There's nothing like going to bed at night with a clear conscience. If you have been silent about your sin, put an end to it today. God's mercies are new every morning.

The fear of man lays a snare, but whoever trusts in the Lord is safe. Many seek the face of a ruler, but it is from the Lord that a man gets justice. An unjust man is an abomination to the righteous, but one whose way is straight is an abomination to the wicked.

Proverbs 29:25-27 ESV

People can hurt us, and at times we can feel afraid of other humans. But if we are fearful of people because we don't want to lose their approval, compromising what we know to be true, we have failed. Even though men may hate us, our trust and hope must remain in God. He will vindicate his children in the end. Some are tempted to cower before others in hope of gaining favor as a result, but God alone brings true justice. God's authority surpasses the power of any king, ruler, leader, or judge. We are called to embrace all people, including those from different ethnicities and economic statues, but the righteous do not have to compromise with those who are evil. The wicked detest the aroma of the Lord in his followers, and the righteous are grieved by the thinking and practice of the ungodly. This animosity will continue until the end. Boldly stand against darkness today.

The words of Agur son of Jakeh. The oracle. The man declares, I am weary, O God; I am weary, O God, and worn out. Surely I am too stupid to be a man. I have not the understanding of a man. I have not learned wisdom, nor have I knowledge of the Holy One.

Proverbs 30:1-3 ESV

The prophet Agur declares the inspired words of the Lord as he confesses from experience that without God he could not attain wisdom. He became exhausted in his quest to discover the meaning of life apart from God's revelation. Life is short, and without God, there is no absolute right or absolute wrong. The honest sage admitted his inability to fabricate an actual purpose for his time on earth. Without a creator, everything, even morality, is relative and subject to change. At the same time, Agur came to the place of fundamental wisdom, realizing that true knowledge comes from the Lord. Human opinions will come and go. Values in fashion today may be out of fashion tomorrow. Where do you turn for wisdom and knowledge? Do you rely upon the opinions of others, or even yourself, or do you follow what God has revealed through the Bible? Seek the Scripture for guidance today.

Who has ascended to heaven and come down? Who has gathered the wind in his fists? Who has wrapped up the waters in a garment? Who has established all the ends of the earth? What is his name, and what is his son's name? Surely you know!

Every word of God proves true; he is a shield to those who take refuge in him. Do not add to his words, lest he rebuke you and you be found a liar.

Proverbs 30:4-6 ESV

Agur declares the vast difference between the lowliness of humanity and the greatness of God. The Lord alone can ascend and descend into heaven, the Lord alone is in control of the weather, and the Lord alone possesses the ability to create from nothing. Genuine wisdom comes from God, who holds absolute power. Every word revealed to man through the Holy Scripture is pure and true, without fault or defect. Those who put their hope in him are preserved through death. In the past, God communicated through his prophets, and then by his Son. His revelation to us is complete, and the canon of Scripture is closed. The one who adds to God's words, no matter how sincere, is a liar. Many have declared that the Lord has new words for his people. Don't listen to them. Stick with the message that was once for all delivered to the saints.

Two things I ask of you; deny them not to me before I die: Remove far from me falsehood and lying; give me neither poverty nor riches; feed me with the food that is needful for me, lest I be full and deny you and say, "Who is the Lord?" or lest I be poor and steal and profane the name of my God.

Proverbs 30:7-9 ESV

The author, Agur, asked the Lord for protection and help regarding two specific things before he died: to be kept from deceit and to be graced with daily needs. Agur was aware of the temptations that can result from having too little or too much. When one struggles to exist, she may be driven to steal. When one becomes too wealthy, she may cease depending upon the Lord. The author considered what would bring most glory to God. He didn't ask for wisdom to manage riches, but for moderation to walk consistently as a follower of the Lord. If he sinned, he would bring shame to the reputation of God and his people, and if he were full, he might ignore the Lord. What are you asking God for in prayer? Do you request that God would give you whatever would bring most glory to his name? Or are you seeking your own glory today?

Do not slander a servant to his master, lest he curse you, and you be held guilty. There are those who curse their fathers and do not bless their mothers. There are those who are clean in their own eyes but are not washed of their filth.

Proverbs 30:10-12 ESV

It is unwise to meddle in the affairs of others. If you speak falsely about someone else's family member, trying to elevate your own reputation, you will suffer. Disrespectful children bring much grief to their families, and not to bless your mother, or to curse your father, are unreasonably cruel behaviors. Some believe they are pure before the Lord, without need of repentance and faith in Christ. They see the world through their own ethical lens. The things they practice are right, and the things they don't practice are wrong. Even if they concede that God is holy and just, they excuse the sinful practices they embrace as negotiable to the Lord. They are convinced that if God exists, he will end up accepting them into his kingdom because they are relatively good. Don't be deceived. Make sure you come to God on his terms and not your own.

There are those—how lofty are their eyes, how high their eyelids lift! There are those whose teeth are swords, whose fangs are knives, to devour the poor from off the earth, the needy from among mankind.

Proverbs 30:13-14 ESV

The arrogant find no need for God, and often see themselves as superior to other people. The proud use their words as harmful weapons to destroy the weak. They lie and manipulate, even giving false testimony in court, to take what little resources the poor have, while hoarding their assets up for themselves. As a result, the less fortunate are no longer able to care for themselves and die prematurely. But God is opposed to these haughty, self-seeking, and devious people. Although the egotistical view themselves as more important than their neighbors, God sees all and will punish their pride. The arrogant think they are wise, powerful, and beautiful, but in God's eyes, they are violent beasts. Choose to humble yourself, asking God to help you see the way he sees today. You may be quite surprised to discover that compared to others, you're not as great as you thought.

*The leech has two daughters: Give and Give.
Three things are never satisfied; four never
say, "Enough": Sheol, the barren womb, the
land never satisfied with water, and the
fire that never says, "Enough."*

Proverbs 30:15-16 ESV

Ancient documents contain warnings about the dangers of the horseleech. This parasite lived in stagnant waters, and when a horse drank, the leech moved inside the animal's nostrils. The leech possessed sucking organs on both ends of its body; with one side it attached itself, and with the other, it drew blood. The leech's sucking organs are the daughters, Give and Give. In the same way, the greedy person sucks the life and resources from her community. Four things are never full or satisfied: the grave, which continually takes life; the barren womb, which longs for a child; the land, which craves rain; and fire, which loves to destroy. The grave and fire both consume life, while the womb and the land produce life. The struggle between life and death on this planet will continue until the Lord brings all to a close. Don't cater to greedy people, as they will never be satisfied.

December

The eye that mocks a father and scorns to obey a mother will be picked out by the ravens of the valley and eaten by the vultures. Three things are too wonderful for me; four I do not understand: the way of an eagle in the sky, the way of a serpent on a rock, the way of a ship on the high seas, and the way of a man with a virgin.

Proverbs 30:17-19 ESV

The ungodly child despises her parents' wise advice. Because she discards the counsel of her mother and her father, her choices lead to a tragic end. Four of God's created beings live wisely within the parameters allotted them, and the author, Agur, is astonished as he considers their ways. He admires the large bird, effortlessly soaring through the sky; the snake, moving along a rock, yet without legs; the ship, skillfully floating on the powerful sea; and the beauty of the physical union within marriage. The man and the virgin, listed last, draw attention to God's magnificent design for human sexuality. God created sex, and we should not be ashamed of it, yet like any other powerful force, it must be kept within the parameters for which it was intended. When sex leaves the safety of marriage, the results can be disastrous. Elevate God's glorious plan for sexual behavior by rejecting whatever falls outside of his design.

This is the way of an adulteress: she eats and wipes her mouth and says, "I have done no wrong."

Proverbs 30:20 ESV

In contrast to the wonderful ways of the bird, the snake, the ship, and the man with his new bride, stands the adulteress. Although she's married and has entered into a sacred covenant with her husband, she still engages in sexual activity with other men. The adulteress doesn't care about the welfare of her targets or her own family. After she eats, or commits the sexual act, she wipes her mouth, hiding all evidence of her deed. Because her conscience is numb, she declares that she has done nothing wrong, reasoning that no one was "hurt" by her actions. Like the adulteress, we may rationalize our own sinful ways, insisting that because there are no clear victims, there's no harm done. But all sin is destructive. Just as far-reaching ripples are created from a stone tossed into water, so sin generates destructive effects on the transgressor, her family, and her community. No one sins alone.

Under three things the earth trembles; under four it cannot bear up: a slave when he becomes king, and a fool when he is filled with food; an unloved woman when she gets a husband, and a maidservant when she displaces her mistress.

Proverbs 30:21-23 ESV

The author lists four things that disrupt social order on the planet. The first is a slave who comes to power. The Hebrew word used here describes not the ordinary slave, but one whom the king trusted. The slave usurped the king's authority and set himself up as ruler over the nation. He caused the downfall of the people and could not be tolerated. The second, a fool who is rewarded with food, becomes arrogant, believing his idiotic ways are prospering. Third is an ungodly and bitter woman who is taken as a man's wife. Last is the female servant who drives out her mistress, probably by seducing her mistress's husband. When unqualified people end up in positions of authority, the community suffers. Do you covet the success of another woman? If so, stop and repent today. Be satisfied with what God has graced you with rather than seeking what isn't truly yours.

Four things on earth are small, but they are exceedingly wise: the ants are a people not strong, yet they provide their food in the summer; the rock badgers are a people not mighty, yet they make their homes in the cliffs;

Proverbs 30:24-26 ESV

Four of God's creatures are quite small yet exercise much wisdom. The first are the tiny ants. Although they clearly have no might over their enemies or the forces of nature that stand against them, they cleverly work together as a community and have food year round. They also recognize that the time is coming when they will not have access to the same resources they have today, and they prepare for the difficult days ahead. The second, the small badger, lives among the rocks. This animal has suction type discs on the pads of its feet to keep it from slipping and falling. Even though they don't have strength, these creatures remain safe by shrewdly employing the tools they have been given for survival and dwelling in a place where their enemies aren't able to live. What gifts or resources has God given you? Use what you have to maximize your efficiency for the God's kingdom today.

the locusts have no king, yet all of them march in rank; the lizard you can take in your hands, yet it is in kings' palaces.

Proverbs 30:27-28 ESV

Agur continues his list with the third and fourth of God's creatures that live wisely despite their insignificant size. The locusts work together as a group, demonstrating the power found in numbers. Although these insects have no official leader, when banded together as a unit, their force is unstoppable. The small wall lizard can be found crawling throughout homes in Israel. Human hands readily snatch it up, but when the lizard makes good choices, it can survive even in the king's palace. The one who lives uprightly can also enjoy the benefits of this life, though vulnerable, by living wisely. Like the locusts, Christians have no supreme earthly leader and yet are all united under the same God and Father. If we determine to overlook our differences, joining with one another to fight darkness rather than bickering among ourselves, we can make a tremendous difference for the kingdom of Christ on this planet.

*Three things are stately in their tread;
four are stately in their stride: the lion,
which is mightiest among beasts and does
not turn back before any; the strutting
rooster, the he-goat, and a king whose
army is with him.*

Proverbs 30:29-31 ESV

The author mentions four beings that walk through life with dignity. The lion, framed by its stately mane, is fearless and shrinks before none. In the same way, the rooster and the goat walk with confidence as they live consistently with God's design for their existence. The king, supported by his army and accompanied by the Spirit of the Lord, has nothing to be afraid of. As God's people, we should lovingly look out for the interests of others, limiting our freedoms and liberties while considering what would benefit those around us; yet, at the same time, the Lord does not expect us to cower before man. Our confidence is in God. He is with us, and he will keep us to the end. With the Lord on our side, we need not fear what man can do as we live out his plan for our lives. Boldly and courageously make good and godly decisions today.

If you have been foolish, exalting yourself, or if you have been devising evil, put your hand on your mouth. For pressing milk produces curds, pressing the nose produces blood, and pressing anger produces strife.

Proverbs 30:32-33 ESV

The one who plots to disrupt the existing social structure by putting another down and promoting himself should stop and cease from his scheme. In fact, he should commit to absolute silence regarding his foolish agenda, even putting his hand on his mouth to keep himself from unwise speech. Just as milk is churned to produce butter, so foolish, self-seeking behavior stirs up the community. When force is applied to the nose, bleeding results, and so pressure in any situation causes a breaking point. Agur cautions the prideful upstart to resist his desire to exalt himself as the community is intolerant of the one bent on boasting. Is there an area where you feel slighted, believing those in authority are ripping you off? Make sure your assessment is accurate by seeking the Scripture and advice of godly counselors before you begin your next self-promoting campaign. Otherwise, general discord and personal shame may result.

The words of King Lemuel. An oracle that his mother taught him: What are you doing, my son? What are you doing, son of my womb? What are you doing, son of my vows? Do not give your strength to women, your ways to those who destroy kings

Proverbs 31:1-3 ESV

Proverbs 31, the final chapter in the book, contains the wisdom of King Lemuel, imparted to him by his mother. Although royal women had influence upon their families and the politics of the day, it is not common to stumble upon an ancient mother's advice to her noble son. Lemuel's mother, the queen, requests that her son make wise decisions and lead well. She reminds her son of his origin from her womb and the vows she made to the Lord concerning him, possibly prior to his conception. The queen begins by imploring her son to avoid entanglement with the wrong women. If he is to lead well, he must limit his sexual behavior. Throughout history, men and women have made destructive decisions based upon ungodly lusts. Sex outside of marriage has ruined empires, families, and even individual lives. God created the gift of sex and calls us to trust him with the constraints he places upon its power.

It is not for kings, O Lemuel, it is not for kings to drink wine, or for rulers to take strong drink, lest they drink and forget what has been decreed and pervert the rights of all the afflicted.

Proverbs 31:4-5 ESV

King Lemuel's mother continues to instruct her son so that he might lead with wisdom. The queen advises him to turn away from the desire to overindulge in alcohol. If intoxicated, the king might ignore justice, even taking advantage of the poor entrusted to his care. The king must be alert, ready to rule rightly over his realm at all times. In the same way, all who walk wisely should exercise extreme caution when drinking alcohol. The righteous one must be continually ready to do the work of the Lord and should never be found "checking out." Would you feel comfortable giving godly counsel or praying after a few drinks? What about those around you who may struggle with an addiction to alcohol? Will your participation embolden them to partake of something they should reject all together? Don't allow alcohol to create distance between you and the Lord, cloud your judgment, or stumble others today.

Give strong drink to the one who is perishing, and wine to those in bitter distress; let them drink and forget their poverty and remember their misery no more.

Proverbs 31:6-7 ESV

King Lemuel's mother imparts further wisdom to her son, again concerning the use of alcohol. In contrast to the instruction she gave to Lemuel personally, the queen suggests that those who are in agony be given strong drink. Although kings and leaders should avoid overconsumption of alcohol, the drink could be useful to the woman who has no hope. The queen is not advising that those who are suffering get away from their problems by turning to drunkenness, nor is she suggesting that those in pain sedate themselves into a stupor. But instead, by revealing that the only time intoxication is an option is when one has lost all hope, she reveals that getting drunk is completely foolish and inappropriate for her son. The woman who is on her deathbed may need help with her pain, but those who are healthy have no justifiable need to escape.

Open your mouth for the mute, for the rights of all who are destitute. Open your mouth, judge righteously, defend the rights of the poor and needy.

Proverbs 31:8-9 ESV

The wise queen instructs her son to use his authority and position to advocate for those who are poor, with no real voice. To "open one's mouth" means to speak up on behalf of someone or something. Due to a lack of financial resources, education, or skill, those who are less fortunate often have a difficult time defending themselves. God is no respecter of persons, and all humans, despite their social or economic status have equal value in his sight. In an affluent culture, it's easy to think that those who are poor or oppressed just don't know any better, and brush their needs and desires off as not that important. We tend to elevate a person's significance in proportion to his bank account. Although those with money can often return the favor when we look out for their interests, the gracious woman is a champion of justice, motivated by a genuine love for God and others.

An excellent wife who can find? She is far more precious than jewels. The heart of her husband trusts in her, and he will have no lack of gain. She does him good, and not harm, all the days of her life.

Proverbs 31:10-12 ESV

The Hebrew word translated "excellent," *hayil*, is a military term, denoting bravery, strength and might. The question "Who can find her?" challenges the reader to search for and become this type of person. The question reveals that this woman is rare, and her worth is far above costly jewels. This fearless woman is of great value to her husband. He has full confidence in her reliability. Interestingly, the Scripture forbids putting trust in anyone other than the Lord, except here. The godly woman is elevated because she fears the Lord, and so her husband can depend upon her. The Hebrew word for "gain," *shalal*, is another military term, describing the spoils of war. Her noble actions are not just for a week, or a month, or even a year; she is an asset to her husband all the days of her life. Let others see you as a woman who believes marriage is for life and for good.

She seeks wool and flax, and works with willing hands. She is like the ships of the merchant; she brings her food from afar. She rises while it is yet night and provides food for her household and portions for her maidens.

Proverbs 31:13-15 ESV

In the ancient Near East, the two primary sources of textile production were wool and flax. This woman weighed, combed, and washed the wool, and she collected, cleaned, and dried the flax, exerting much hard and painstaking labor. Even though she had money, she didn't turn from vigorous toil. Her hard work resulted in fabrics to be sold in the marketplace. People spent large amounts of money to acquire the best clothing. She used her resources to purchase exquisite and rare foods for her household. The Hebrew word translated as "food" actually refers to the prey of wild animals. The author's word choice provides a parallel between our woman and a lioness. The lioness hunts through the dark hours to provide her cubs with prey. This woman doesn't stay up all night, but she is as aggressive as the lioness, taking care of her household. Will you choose to put the needs of your family before your own today?

She considers a field and buys it; with the fruit of her hands she plants a vineyard. She dresses herself with strength and makes her arms strong.

Proverbs 31:16-17 ESV

She thinks of strategic ways to invest the money she's earned from her textile business. She strategically considers the best financial course of action and creates a plan. She doesn't stop with a proposal. After praying and planning, she buys a field. With her own hands, she clears the dirt of rocks before she plants a vineyard. Her hands, or palms, prepared and processed the wool and flax, and now expand her wealth by investing into a vineyard. Although this woman has servants, she is disposed to do the work of a servant. Whether physically or spiritually, she's always set to do whatever the Lord requires of her to be useful to him. Are you wiling to do manual, even humble labor? Or do you see yourself as above certain jobs or roles? Be prepared to do whatever God asks of you today.

> She perceives that her merchandise is profitable. Her lamp does not go out at night. She puts her hands to the distaff, and her hands hold the spindle. She opens her hand to the poor and reaches out her hands to the needy.

Proverbs 31:18-20 ESV

Her work makes a difference in the community. In the ancient Near East, the well ordered home had a lamp burning all through the night as a sign of the household's success. When the lamp went out, all would know the home experienced poverty. This woman is successful because she labors without any signs of complaining, murmuring, or muttering. Her palms grasp the spindle, which was used to create useful and strong threads from her prepared materials. She skillfully and intelligently holds her tools, manipulating them to create superior products for her household while generating extra income. She invites the less fortunate to enjoy her wealth, and she blesses them with material goods. This woman realizes that her prosperity is a gift from God, and even though she labors continually, she is always eager and willing to share. Are you tight-fisted when it comes to the poor around you? Are you willing to be generous today?

She is not afraid of snow for her household, for all her household are clothed in scarlet. She makes bed coverings for herself; her clothing is fine linen and purple. Her husband is known in the gates when he sits among the elders of the land.

Proverbs 31:21-23 ESV

Because she has worked to provide the best supplies for her family, including wool clothes for the winter months, she isn't afraid of the coming cold. Although the approaching harsh months of winter generated fear and anxiety in the unprepared, she is calm and at ease, realizing that those under her care have what's necessary to endure the severe months ahead. Scarlet or crimson wool represented expensive fabrics, and purple dye was quite costly, so it was considered a luxury to enjoy these fabrics. Although she is continually busy, meeting the needs of others, she makes herself look good for her husband. When her husband comes home, he doesn't worry about picking up where she left off. Her man has time to engage in the affairs of the people. Do you empower others to do what they normally couldn't? Or do you squeeze every minute out of your spouse, so that he's got nothing left to give to the Lord?

She makes linen garments and sells them; she delivers sashes to the merchant. Strength and dignity are her clothing, and she laughs at the time to come.

Proverbs 31:24-25 ESV

She creates all sorts of beautiful garments and sells them in the marketplace, enhancing the status of her household. Although we may not be merchandising clothing, we are all called to labor. Even if you aren't employed outside the home, you can enrich the reputation of your family by being known for loving and serving others as you invest in your church. This woman covers herself with strength and dignity, known by all to be faithful, diligent, and kind, focusing on others and trusting in the Lord. She is not afraid of the future, including unforeseen and potential difficulties. In fact, like a victorious warrior, she laughs triumphantly at the days to come. She is confident that God will properly manage the affairs of her life. Are you fearful of the future, worried that the Lord will forsake you? Or are you boldly trusting in him to successfully move you from one day to the next?

She opens her mouth with wisdom, and the teaching of kindness is on her tongue. She looks well to the ways of her household and does not eat the bread of idleness. Her children rise up and call her blessed; her husband also, and he praises her.

Proverbs 31:26-28 ESV

Again, to "open one's mouth" was a phrase the Hebrews used to explain the ability to speak thoroughly and effectively to the concerns of those who come to the godly woman for counsel. Her wisdom results from a lifetime of putting the truth of God's word into practice. The woman who has immersed herself in God's grace is quick to extend grace to others. "Looking well to" means that something is being watched over carefully. This woman carefully watches over the affairs of her home, ready to adjust whenever change is necessary. She invests into the physical, emotional, and spiritual growth of her children, and she is a trusted companion for her husband. The family applauds the mother and wife as one to look up to. Do you desire to have others look up to you as a good and godly model? By confidently trusting in God, working hard, and investing in others, you will be admired and commended too.

"Many women have done excellently, but you surpass them all." Charm is deceitful, and beauty is vain, but a woman who fears the Lord is to be praised. Give her of the fruit of her hands, and let her works praise her in the gates.

Proverbs 31:29-31 ESV

The husband declares with confidence that she is the most excellent of all women. This poem, defining the valiant wife or woman, uses the language of heroic poetry. Beauty lasts a short period of time, and it always promises far more than it delivers. Although it is important to invest in our appearance, managing the bodies God has entrusted us with and satisfying our husbands sexually, beauty is nevertheless fleeting. The key to the excellent wife's success is her fear of the Lord. Her life's work, the fruit of her hands, leave a legacy like that of a victorious warrior, who diligently and courageously risks her own well being in order to benefit the circumstances of those around her. She lives fearlessly, trusting in God over men, knowing that the Lord will accomplish all that he intends through her obedient choices. Decide to become a woman God chooses to use for his glory and the good of others today.

Selected Bibliography

Waltke, Bruce K. 2004. *The Book of Proverbs: Chapters 1-15*. Grand Rapids, MI: Wm. B. Eerdmans Publishing Company.

— . 2005. *The Book of Proverbs: Chapters 15-31*. Grand Rapids, MI: Wm. B. Eerdmans Publishing Company.